T0323995

Cambridge Elements

Elements in Historical Theory and Practice
edited by
Daniel Woolf
Queen's University, Ontario

PRAGMATISM AND HISTORICAL REPRESENTATION

Serge Grigoriev
Ithaca College

Shaftesbury Road, Cambridge CB2 8EA, United Kingdom

One Liberty Plaza, 20th Floor, New York, NY 10006, USA

477 Williamstown Road, Port Melbourne, VIC 3207, Australia

314–321, 3rd Floor, Plot 3, Splendor Forum, Jasola District Centre,
New Delhi – 110025, India

103 Penang Road, #05–06/07, Visioncrest Commercial, Singapore 238467

Cambridge University Press is part of Cambridge University Press & Assessment,
a department of the University of Cambridge.

We share the University's mission to contribute to society through the pursuit of
education, learning and research at the highest international levels of excellence.

www.cambridge.org
Information on this title: www.cambridge.org/9781009533577

DOI: 10.1017/9781009053280

When citing this work, please include a reference to the DOI 10.1017/9781009053280

First published 2024

A catalogue record for this publication is available from the British Library

ISBN 978-1-009-53357-7 Hardback
ISBN 978-1-009-05510-9 Paperback
ISSN 2634-8616 (online)
ISSN 2634-8608 (print)

Pragmatism and Historical Representation

Elements in Historical Theory and Practice

DOI: 10.1017/9781009053280
First published online: November 2024

Serge Grigoriev
Ithaca College

Author for correspondence: Serge Grigoriev, sgrigoriev@ithaca.edu

Abstract: No prominent pragmatist philosopher to date has offered us a fully developed theory of history or historical interpretation. Nevertheless, a number of pivotal arguments and suggestions made by the pragmatists appeared to many both insightful and pertinent enough to offer a distinctive promise of a cohesive and distinctive general pragmatist perspective in historical theory. The present contribution is intended to secure some advances in this direction, focusing on the relationships between objectivity and perspective; between representation as an accurate correspondence to reality and the social, cultural sense of representation as being represented and being representative; as well as the relationship between individualizing comprehension and generalizing abstraction in historical contexts.

Keywords: pragmatism, history, representation, objectivity, pluralism

ISBNs: 9781009533577 (HB), 9781009055109 (PB), 9781009053280 (OC)
ISSNs: 2634-8616 (online), 2634-8608 (print)

Contents

Introduction

One common way to describe pragmatism is simply to refer the reader to the intellectual tradition originating in the writings of three classical pragmatists (C.S. Peirce, William James, and John Dewey) and the associated figures, revived and reinterpreted at the close of the twentieth century by authors like Richard Rorty and Hilary Putnam, among others. This minimal characterization, however, can be profoundly reductive and misleading, both with respect to the past history of pragmatism and with respect to its contemporary scope: its inspiration, sources, and affinities. Despite the overlapping, often shared, lines of intellectual descent, when it comes to their principal themes and commitments, most pragmatists emphatically resist the notion that their tradition can be circumscribed by some enumeration of canonical figures or classical lines of argument. Instead, they pride themselves on the commitment to a perpetual renewal of the tradition: through examining the previously neglected strands of the tradition itself, through engagement with the competing philosophical traditions, and through maintaining a constant awareness and sensitivity to the evolving and emergent concerns of the larger social, and cultural discourse. There is, at present, no shortage of excellent publications offering sometimes competing accounts of what pragmatism is: from rigorous and analytically focused *Cambridge Pragmatism* by Cheryl Misak to the richly contextualized pluralism of Albert Spencer's *American Pragmatism: an Introduction*, with simultaneously concise and nuanced middle-of-the-road entries – such as Michael Bacon's *Pragmatism: an Introduction* – offering an accessible yet sophisticated route to engaging with many of the pragmatism's core figures and defining themes.

The present essay harbors no pretense of describing pragmatism as a whole, or even of addressing every pragmatist vision and contribution pertinent to its subject matter. Nor does it aim at a systematic exposition of the many interrelated pragmatist-leaning themes in the recent fertile literature on historical theory. It would be presumptuous to attempt either in earnest in the limited space provided. Instead, the essay confines itself to one theme: Outlining a tentative trajectory for a conceptually sustainable transition from the traditional view of representation as an *accurate depiction* of past events towards representation understood as *being represented* – having one's voice, one's perspective, and one's contributions included and properly attended to in the narratives of the past. Taking its initial queue from what sometimes has been referred to as the "crisis of objectivity" at the close of the twentieth century – that is, widespread questioning of the notion of correspondence to untheorized reality as a neutral (and natural) criterion of historical objectivity – it attempts to enlist some familiar conceptual resources of the pragmatist tradition in order to explore the potential promise of replacing the old question, of how history can faithfully represent past reality, with the new question of who and what must be considered *representative* – that is, worthy of historical representation?

Finally, while mining the writings of the respective pragmatist figures for some enabling themes, it will not do to forget that the arguments and the proposals thus borrowed belong conceptually to the complex and intricate fabric of each philosopher's elaborate and individualized vision. It is to be hoped that the abridgment and simplification necessitated by the style and intention of this essay do not result in any substantial distortions or misrepresentations of its source material, provided its obligatory partiality is conceded in advance.

For the present purposes, then, pragmatism can be understood as an attempt to extend the best features of modern scientific thinking to the study of philosophy: focusing on the results rather than first principles; emphasizing testable hypothesis formation and experimental intervention over speculative theorizing. Pragmatism, thus, orients itself towards the exploration of new possibilities and undisclosed potentialities, rather than certainty and putatively unassailable foundations.

Furthermore, pragmatists tend to understand the process of cultural learning and intellectual discovery as quintessentially social, communal, and historically situated. Our pursuit of truth, for a pragmatist, is always motivated, in large part, by a *meliorist* concern – a trust in the possibility of a substantial improvement of life through finite advances in rational understanding and practical engagement. Because of this, pragmatists tend to emphasize the central role of judgment in the constitution of knowledge: Our view is never a view from nowhere; it is enabled and supported by our concrete values and interests.

The content of our encounters with the world is never a mere "given," but is a product of consecutive active attempts to extract some potentially valuable lessons from these encounters. The answers that we find depend on the questions that we pose, conditioned by our problems, our interests, and our resources. Consequently, pragmatists tend to draw attention to the perspectival nature of knowledge and its dependence on the varying aims and regimes of representation. Together, these programmatic commitments or attitudes can serve as a rough conceptual backdrop for the narrative that follows.

Starting the story with Emerson may count as a controversial move. Most would contend that Emerson is not really a pragmatist in the conventional sense;

at best, he is a proto-pragmatist.[1] Nevertheless, all agree that Emerson casts a very long shadow over the subsequent development of pragmatism, serving both as an inspiration and a common source of its many enduring and defining themes. John Dewey's well-known assessment of his foundational role appoints him as the "prophet and herald" of any future democratic conception of philosophy (mw.3.191); and for this reason, if for no other, it seems fitting to begin our own story with the Emersonian claim that what matters intellectually about individual persons and social-cultural situations is their "representative quality" (W 4:8).

For Emerson, history provides the only possible answer to the philosophical problem of self-knowledge: Comprehending the historically developing human potential that expresses itself in the transitions between different forms of life, their conflicts, tensions, and alternatives that they generate. History broadens our self-conception, by suggesting alternatives to our familiar and established ways of organizing our individual and collective existence, supplying thereby a metaphorical articulation of our own present possibilities. Being historically representative, from this perspective, is determined by the revelatory quality of one's being and conduct: A capacity to illuminate the constitutive principles of the conditions under which one labors by responding to them in an intelligent and articulate manner.

Such representative contributions do not usually arise by chance but are an outcome of an active struggle to come to terms with one's historical circumstances, reconfigured as an exemplary historical situation from the perspective of one's articulated representative response. Recounting the characteristic historical episodes constituted in this way contributes, then, to our growing appreciation of the diversity and amplitude of the concretely instantiated, perpetually evolving human potential.

With Dewey, the philosophical interest in historical self-knowledge becomes subordinate to the interest in cultural melioristic self-transformation. In his view, the representative responses that normally originate with specific individuals can rarely be counted upon to produce the desired transformation, unless reprocessed into enduring social-cultural structures and habits, amenable to systematic exposition and intelligent control.

Even so, one always begins by examining the way that historical problems are posed and resolved within the context of concrete individual conflicted (or "indeterminate") situations, pertaining both to historical events and historical research. The key to historical understanding, in Dewey's view, consists in

[1] The difference in the intellectual temper between Emerson and the classical pragmatists being roughly analogous to that between German Romantics and German Idealists in Jena.

the recognition of the "representative character" (mw.4.95) of objects and events – of their capacity to serve as evidence, as signs that point us toward appropriate observations and conclusions.

The grasp of an individual situation, however – or even many such situations – does not translate, on its own, into a systematic theory of historical inquiry that Dewey is after. Attempting the latter transition requires a substantial and practical engagement with the problem of how what is learned in one situation can be transferred to a different situation, raising questions about the role of abstract generalizations in history. How can we use the same concepts to secure understanding across divergent situations, perspectives, and cultural contexts? Is it possible, in fact, that this desire for systematicity is itself misplaced?

That, in fact, is the line advocated by Richard Rorty. Our next chapter begins by recounting his influential critique of the very idea of "correct representation" as "correspondence to reality." Originating in a philosophical fiction, according to Rorty, not only does this notion fail to square with our ordinary pragmatic intuitions about reality and truth, it proves to be (even) philosophically incoherent. Reality certainly imposes constraints on our theories: but these constraints are causal, and can be coherently interpreted in different ways. We cannot compare verbal theories or descriptions to reality: only to other theories and descriptions that appear superior (or not) in the light of our practical, causal encounters with the world.

Rorty's own response to this critical realization, however, has been received with considerably less enthusiasm than his critique. While sharing Dewey's and Emerson's concern with cultural representation and possibilities of self-transformation, Rorty deliberately resists advancing any systematic criteria for selecting the more promising possibilities and perspectives. Novelty and uninhibited experimentation is what really matters. One does not become representative for an assignable reason: one just ends up – retrospectively – representing and being regarded as representative. We can state our preferences and reasons; but cannot compel others to share them.

Rorty's nonchalant encouragement of the imaginative proliferation of alternative perspectives has often met with a critical reception, even among his most sympathetic readers, simply because it appears to erase the line between inventive aesthetic activity and public responsibility, characteristic of the historical discourse. The pragmatist commitment to context-sensitivity and perspectival pluralism may be unsustainable without a balancing strategy for reaching a reasoned intersubjective agreement and finding a common ground between the divergent arguments and perspectives.

Brandom's account of conceptual integration through historical recollection – abridged, in this instance, for the purpose of maintaining both focus and accessibility[2] – offers one plausible model for understanding how intellectual traditions coalesce through the social historical processes of mutual recognition over time, without eliminating the sense of a productive disagreement and contestation within each tradition and in the competition between them.

The conceptual content of our encounters with reality, according to Brandom, is not something that we can actually locate in the experience itself. In fact, our attempts to articulate what reality really *is* must portray it as a modal space of possibilities structured by relations of compatible and incompatible differences, compatible and incompatible descriptions or predications. Because of this, describing reality always entails tracing the inferential relationships that constitute it as a conceptually determinate space.

The progressive articulation of these relationships, in turn, can only be accomplished within the context of a self-correcting intellectual tradition, aspiring to attain an ever greater expressive clarity concerning its subject matter, without claiming the impossible privileged access to the untheorized reality independent of our historically developing perspectives. Our present sense of reality, then – including the reality of the past – is always generated through a deliberate integration of valuable past perspectives recognized as properly belonging to its genealogical constitution. An important implication of this view, with respect to our narrative as a whole, will be briefly adumbrated in the conclusion.

1 Emerson: Representing the Human Potential

1.1 History and Human Nature

When invited to consider the idea of history in the most general sense, one may be tempted to imagine it as a big story, a conventional narrative with humanity as the protagonist, undergoing a series of dramatic encounters and collisions. Such is the history of *res gestae*, wherein the identity of the protagonist remains substantially unaltered – despite the accidental properties that temporarily accrue to it as a result of concrete historical circumstances and transactions. Composing such stories implicitly favors the theoretical conception of a (mostly) fixed human nature – a common denominator that constitutes our basic, shared humanity, irrespective of the superficial differences due to the accidents of time and place. As human beings, we do, of course, share many features – including, say, biological and psychological ones – that have

[2] My essay "Pragmatism" in the *Routledge Companion to Historical Theory* as well as "Reason, Language, History" in *Metaphilosophy (2022)* can provide some additional context.

remained virtually invariant throughout history. It seems entirely plausible to claim, for example, that our history has been shaped in considerable part simply by what we can and cannot digest. The shortcoming of such histories is that, to use a popular, hackneyed phrase, they are lacking in "character development."

To wit, the most remarkable feature of our shared nature is that we are, above all, cultural beings – possessed of the capacity and need to spontaneously internalize a language and a cultural form of life fairly early on in the process of normal development. Moreover, every one of us is capable (at least in theory) of internalizing any one of the bewilderingly diverse spectrum of cultural and linguistic forms and possibilities made available by history, acquiring, in the process, a pronouncedly distinctive type of cultural identity. Attaining maturity within a particular historical cultural constellation tends to render us progressively more inflexible – locked into the specific options favored by our concrete historical experience; but the nature of humanity itself always remains essentially plastic – and capable, on that score, of indefinite growth and self-transformation. Considered from this angle, the history of humanity becomes a kind of *Bildungsroman* – a history of the discovery and unfolding of the ever-broader spectrum of human potentialities. This latter view of history happens to be the one favored by Emerson and the pragmatists who were influenced by him.

"History is the record of what men are," Emerson writes, "is the record of the character of the human race" (EL2, 129). The "true history of man" (EL2, 63), in his view, is contained in *literature*, understood in the "largest sense," as that which attempts to "*give voice to the whole of spiritual nature* as events and ages unfold it" (EL1, 226). Its intention is to provide us with the "portraiture of man" (Richardson 1995, 190) conceived simultaneously as "history" (of what once has been possible) and "prophecy" (of what may be possible yet, perhaps – once again). History, in other words, contributes to our conception of the human nature, understood in the dynamic, historical terms of the perpetually unfolding and developing human potential. On the one hand, this approach to history can be imagined on the analogy with art history: tracing the invention, flourishing, and fading of new styles, new themes, new visions, new techniques, and new value schemes. On the other, it can be compared to the study of natural history, with its episodes of novel emergence, proliferation, extinction and decline, situated within a dynamic evolutionary perspective, wherein the significance of each episode becomes amplified in the light of its contribution to the lines of growth and descent that transcend its own narrow temporal frame. It is a history of transitions between different forms of life: New types of unity, order, and meaning discoverable by the human mind searching for promising alternatives to the already familiar and established ways of organizing our individual and collective existence.

It is sometimes said that Emerson inverted the organic theories of history popular in his day, with their tendency to "merge the individual into the process of history" (EL2, 3),[3] by absorbing all of history into the central figure of a living individual. The function of history, in his view, was to be injected into the mind so as to direct and energize its inner processes, enabling it to uncover and rehearse its own hidden possibilities, disclosed and realized by other human beings in the past. Because of this, history needed to find a way to resonate with its intended audience: The narrative "must correspond to something in me to be credible" (EL2, 13). One general strategy to accomplish this was to present historical developments as the product and outcome of human thought and feeling in the broadest sense: unless "explained from individual history," all history "must remain words" (EL2, 19).

Emerson is prone to deliberate exaggeration but, while his contention certainly doesn't capture the entire breadth of legitimate historical concerns, it also provides us with one straightforward motivation to study history. History, on his view, provides the only adequate solution to the philosophical problem of self-knowledge. As human beings, we always remain partially opaque to ourselves: "our own life we cannot subject to the eye of the intellect" (EL2, 16). But, standing before great pictures of history "we can practice our eyes and judgments better" (EL2, 181). We thus learn to concern ourselves with "the history and destiny of a man; whilst the cloud of egotists drifting about are only interested in a success to their egotism"; with this anthropocentric broadening of our intellectual horizons, finally permitting a person to "see himself as an object," a passing element of the universal, multifaceted humanity (W 12:39).

Yet, to accomplish this, history must be written as a history of human nature – "this human nature of mine" (EL2, 16). Conceiving human nature, in turn, as the progressively expanding horizon of realized human potentialities sets up, for Emerson, a historical dynamic relationship between the actual and the potential, the *actual* and the *ideal*, mediated by the notion of *growth* (Whicher 1953, 141 & 143) towards the "unattained but attainable self" (W 2:7) suggested in the very idea of a universal human potential, cogently maintained alongside the acceptance of the actual "tragic limitations of human history" (Robinson 1993, 77).

If one of the principal motivations for studying history is to discover among its materials and records some instances of analogical or metaphorical

[3] The observation is made by the editors (S. Whicher, R. Spiller, and W. Williams) in an untitled prefatory note to one of the sections in the volume, without an individual attribution.

articulation and indication of our own present possibilities, then coming to embody novel possibilities of living must constitute a paradigmatic historical achievement for both individuals and social groups. In fact, Emerson insists that the significance of a human life consists primarily in its "pictorial or representative quality" (W 4:8; W 3:225) and, therefore, "the production of a life that eloquently manifests one's character" (Lysaker 2008, 55) can be regarded as a cardinal duty, both to ourselves and to posterity.

Character, moreover, in this context, must be understood as a set of operational regularities, entrenched affinities for putting things into a certain kind of "right order" (LLR2, 161). Every human being is a *classifier* after a manner of her own (LLR2, 163), and while the immediate results of our enterprises eventually dissolve into oblivion, the *principles* which guide our activities – our ordering of priorities, our reasoning strategies, our distinctive styles of perceiving the world – endure (LLR2, 113 & 115) and can be successfully redeployed under an endless variety of altered circumstances. Their value consists, in part, in their individual quality: stemming from a sense of an inner compulsion or felt necessity, similar to the one that guides an artist in determining what is missing in the painting's composition. Yet, what is disclosed in this individual fashion are objective possibilities, working relationships: "to make anything useful or beautiful, the individual must be submitted to the universal mind" (EL2, 44). "Subjectiveness," according to Emerson, is simply a new name for "intellectual selfishness" (EL3, 214). "The great," he goes on, "always introduce us to facts; small men introduce us always to themselves" (EL3, 215). The function of the individual style, then, consists simply in rendering perspicuous what otherwise may remain opaque; the individuality is expressive – and representative – in a way that the principles and facts which secure its operation are usually not.

Being representative, then, consists in being able to illustrate, in a compelling and exemplary fashion, the heretofore unexamined aspects of the historically developing human potential. The fact that human nature remains everywhere substantially the same does not imply that its concrete manifestations are either uniform or mutually interchangeable. Water remains everywhere the same; yet it displays very different characteristics as snow, as ice, as steam, as a running stream, a wave, as a liquid that we drink or drown in. Similarly, human nature can express itself in a wide range of distinctive paradigmatic phenomena. In doing so it sometimes sets a self-perpetuating precedent; and sometimes merely affords us a glimpse of an elusive possibility, nearly impossible to replicate. Whatever is representative succeeds in rendering perspicuous some common mechanisms, principles, and qualities of interest.

In this regard, the statistical average, a generic representative, can rarely be representative in the required sense. The ability to *stand in* for a category or a group as a fair sample bears no determinate relationship to being able to express or show what the category actually *stands for*: to disclose the distinguishing principles of its characteristic modes of operation. For example, an average storyteller may not be the best candidate to assist in developing a sophisticated grasp of the complex strategies of dramatic narration. The emphasis on the close study of what is perspicuously representative, as opposed to the merely common, distinguishes a philosophical approach to history from the "mere annalist and fact-monger" approach (EL2, 179): It teaches us to intuit and hypothesize relationships and possibilities of general importance from a limited but strategically chosen sample. We can learn more about the Roman architecture from an intent examination of one exemplary building than from an indifferent survey of a hundred.

It is an approach congenial to Jacob Burckhardt's concern with the "typical" as opposed to the "realistic figures" (Burckhardt 1979, 114), focused upon developing an inventory of the "ideal forms" characteristic of specific historical periods and forms of life (Burckhardt 1979, 275). The sense of "ideal," in this case, is strictly specific and pluralistic: Every representative figure is partial – "we must cease to look in men for completeness" (W 4:34). Moreover, it is purely epistemic and aesthetic: An interest in representative expressiveness must not be attended by a moralizing intention – every condition has its defects and compensations (EL2, 153), and being objectionable doesn't render it any less interesting, or any less a part of the human potential.

Despite not being average, an outstanding representative character is valuable precisely because it clarifies something common, exhibiting "common faculties under a bias" (EL2, 100). As pragmatist historians of culture, we are interested primarily in the "common and natural motions of the soul, what the cook, the peasant, and the soldier say" (EL1, 165), in the possibilities that lie close at hand for the many, not the few. Hence, only those protagonists are truly great and interesting "whose characters are easy to understand, and with whom we feel intimately acquainted" (EL1, 119), since in their individual conduct we can plainly discern what remains arrested, concealed, attenuated, and distorted in others. Being representative, then, also manifests itself in the spontaneous capacity to relate to a wide spectrum of human personalities and concerns, but after a distinctive individual manner of one's own. (Emerson is concerned first and foremost with individuals; but the same considerations could apply *mutatis mutandis* to artifacts, institutions, and practices.) In representativeness we seek for a uniquely characteristic response to typical conditions.

As John Lysaker put it "the self of self-culture is not just me, or even solely mine, but it is intertwined with others" (Lysaker 2008, 27). One of Emerson's principal enduring preoccupations was "to reground the culture of the self in the moral texture of social life" (Robinson 1993, 136). An individual might be a laboratory for experimenting with new thoughts, new modes of conduct, new forms of cultural life, but she draws her materials from her concrete historical situatedness, which she must accept as her territory, no matter how inauspicious – "the society of our contemporaries, the connexion of events" (W 2:47). Representativeness requires great powers of receptivity; and, at times, the inventive power "consists in not being original at all; in being altogether receptive; in letting the world do all, and suffering the spirit of the hour to pass unobstructed through the mind" (W 4:191).

One succeeds in representing the cultural situation only by responding to its challenges and opportunities on the terms that it offers. The important point is not to express oneself, but to *answer*, in a characteristic manner of one's own. It is impossible to offer anything of historical interest without being a participant in the life of humanity, without taking up a distinctive position vis-à-vis the others. The development of an original individual style depends upon hearing other voices, both the ones that one finds internally persuasive and those that one rejects or resists. We participate in the cultural life by conversing with significant ideas and practices, interpreting them, and contributing to the definition of their meaning. We address others who brought one into the conversation; borrowing their words; addressing their problems; and contesting their results.

"Every master has found his materials collected," Emerson observes, "and his power lay in his sympathy with his people and in his love of the materials he wrought in. What an economy of power! and what a compensation for the shortness of life! All is done to his hand" (W 4:190). This, of course, does not imply an unconditional endorsement of the terms on which the cultural discourse and social policy are presently conducted: One accepts the situation for what it is, but embraces only what is "affirmative" in it – "by the choice of what is positive, of what is advancing" (LLR2, 126). A discerning mind scrutinizes the present for its healthy tendencies, which it resolves to follow; and, in doing so, inadvertently contributes to their advancement.

The past episodes of representative living serve as "lenses through which we read our own minds" (W 4:5), uncovering our own latent potentialities. Because of this, history calls for readers who can read it "actively," as a commentary upon and an elucidation of their own life (EL2, 182). Only for such an audience can collecting the "fragments of the centuries" become a vital pursuit (EL2, 186), intimately connected to the philosophical project of obtaining self-knowledge. Naturally, our capacity for historical comprehension is not unlimited: A mind retains well only what is congenial to its own nature and manner of thought (W 2:144).

"A mind," writes Emerson, "does not receive truth as a chest receives jewels that are put into it, but as the stomach takes up food into the system" (W 12:32–33). It is a question of what can be properly absorbed and utilized: "he has it who can use it" (W 12:32–33). However, the process of historical cultural education is a twofold process. On the one hand, it allows its students to develop a sense of their own unique perspective, their style of engaging with the shared cultural space; on the other, it broadens the horizon of our capacity for meaningful response, with the (perhaps unattainable) ideal being that of a mind that feels itself "addressed in every event of the past" (EL2, 16).

Emerson's focus on the uniquely individualized manner of representative responses should not obscure this important correlative dimension of *decentering* that characterizes genuine intellectual growth. "Man," Emerson insists, "is powerful only by the multitude of his affinities" (EL2, 17); his strength "consists not in his properties but in his innumerable relations" (EL2, 155). His notable conception of abandonment – as a path towards transcending one's present settled loyalties and convictions – appears, on the positive side, to initiate a transition towards new interests, new commitments, and new possibilities of attachment. As a result, we learn to play different roles, engage with different environments, and occupy different points of view.

If "a man fasten on a single aspect of truth," Emerson warns, "and apply himself to that alone for a long time, the truth becomes distorted and not itself, but falsehood" (W 2:339), simply because it eclipses the fact of its own partiality. Certainly, "people wish to be settled"; but "only as far as they are unsettled is there any hope for them" (W 2:320). Complacency spells the death of an active intellect. Hence, the search for the new perspectives, new values, new points of departure – which proceeds by at least an initial abandonment or suspension of the established affinities, verities, and points of view – can itself be interpreted as a search for a greater inclusiveness, universality, attained through a sequential assumption of potentially incommensurable perspectives, rather than through the arbitrary positing of a logically immaculate coherent whole.

"The truest state of mind rested in," says Emerson, "becomes false" (W 2:320). Our only security against ossified and complacent partiality lies in a constant reevaluation and reconstruction, in the perpetually renewed decentering transitions (W 2:319–20). Because of this, history for Emerson is an essentially progressive discipline, since we can always anticipate that at the "higher stages of being" we might both "remember and understand our early history better" (W 12:102). The more we learn, the more incentives we possess to revisit and reevaluate our past. The "past does not sleep," according to Emerson: "With every new fact a ray of light shoots up from the long buried years" (W 12:101). "Indeed," he muses, "what is our own being but a re-production, a re-presentation of all the past?" (EL3, 251).[4]

1.2 Culture and Society

A character provides us with a perspective: It mediates and configures our comprehension of its cultural, historical world, exposing its animating mechanisms and tensions in their interaction with a concrete individual personality. But isn't this concern with the personal, with representative living a bit naïve? What of the powerful, predominantly impersonal, forces and agencies (political, economic, informational, social) that shape and reshape our collective reality? Emerson does not deny their influence; however, he finds the resulting news of the day both "dubious and melancholy" (EL2, 156). Nor does he entertain any illusions regarding the "feeble influence of thought on life" (JMN 5:489): with the ideal and the actual running almost on parallel tracks, with "no greater disposition to reconcile themselves" in the course of an individual life (JMN, 8:10–11).

Nevertheless, his general attitude of "piety towards Being" (Friedl 2000, 152) prompts Emerson to maintain a qualified trust in the reasonableness of the underlying tendency of the world and history as a whole. Discerning this positive tendency in things, intuited incipiently at the level of an individual experience, provides a starting point for the affirmation of one's historical destiny and place. One would imagine, Emerson intones, that between the self-serving ruthlessness of power and the inertia of the "ignorant and deceivable majority" all things should soon come to ruin (EL2, 75). Yet, they endure; with something new and worthy of our respect and admiration eventually arising; and this happens with an enviable consistency. "All our theories of the progress of man," Emerson says, "are baffled when we come to apply them to actual society" (EL2, 174). Still, simultaneously, cultural advancement creates ever-new opportunities for the enlargement of individual character (W 1:107) and for conceiving different improved possibilities and forms of life, thereby enabling us to have serious and warranted conversations about the "historical progress of man" (EL2, 213).

An historically informed pragmatist orientation compels us to recognize, with Emerson, that the ideas at work in the concrete present – no matter how disagreeable – can be as profound as those associated with "the most illustrious

[4] Hyphenation added for emphasis.

events" (EL2, 159). "Trust the time," Emerson advises, "What a fatal prodigality to contemn *our* age" (EL3, 200). We must model the guiding principles of our character and our practices on those aspects of the past and present experience that we find most promising and admirable; and in doing so, in our own example, we may come to embody certain ideal, anticipatory possibilities of living that may, eventually, form the basis of a significant, influential historical precedent. It is in this "possible influence of character," Emerson argues, that the true "extent of one man" is revealed to the world (EL3, 242). An articulate representative character becomes a template, a formula for a species of cultural life. "The qualities," says Emerson, "abide; the men who exhibit them have now more, now less, and pass away; the qualities remain on another brow" (W 4:33–4). And this "genius of humanity" that provides us with the perpetual opportunities to reinvent ourselves constitutes for Emerson the "right point of view of history" (W 4:33–4).

The growth of culture, for Emerson, is the ideal element in history, with culture itself understood as the "upbuilding of a man" (W 1:107), through the suggestion of an expanded "range of affinities" and possibilities of alternative development, that help us "modulate the violence of any master-tones" predominant in our natural untutored character (W 6:136–7). This idealism, in turn, is premised on the essential historicity of human experience: Everything that is actual is also passing; and things that obstruct our vision today may no longer be there tomorrow. History shows that life is capable of qualitative and radical transformation over time, suggesting the rationality of the refusal to simply reconcile oneself to the "given" conditions of the present: " . . . if history were complete, if history exhausted the possibilities of our nature, if human life were not haunted by hope and faith, – the problem of human life would not remain still to be solved" (EL3, 13).

The true promise of modernity, for Emerson, resided in the dawning recognition of the universal significance of the human spirit embodied in each and every individual (EL2, 68). "The former generations," he writes, "acted under the belief that a shining social prosperity was the aim of men: and sacrificed uniformly individuals to the nation" (EL3, 188), treating individuals as mere "appendages" to state, army, commerce, production (EL2, 214–5). "Culture," for Emerson, is the awkward word meant to signal the new realization of the intrinsic value of our common humanity (EL2, 215). Culture is nothing but the unfolding of the human nature in history (EL2, 215), the successive realization and enrichment of its multiform potentialities. "Man," writes Emerson, "is explicable by nothing less than all his history. Without hurry, without rest, the human spirit goes forth from the beginning to embody every faculty, every thought, every emotion which belongs to it, in appropriate events" (EL2, 13).

A single person, a thinking, feeling individual provides us with a more concrete and complete meaning of what it means to be human than any number of assorted parties, sects, and tribes. A concrete individual "represents not a private but a universal interest" (EL3, 199).

Society, meanwhile, remains a repository of forms, interests, and habits that frequently stand in the way of genuine cultural development. Society, above all else, aspires toward material progress; and its history, as a result, concerns itself mostly with successive redistributions of power and resources. The logic of power, the logic of domination, which animates the conventional (political) history stands in essential opposition to the logic of representation, promoted by a cultural interest in humanity.

Even the best historical narratives in this vein present us with a "barren and wearisome chronicle" which tells us little about humanity proper (EL2, 8). As we read on about the politically conspicuous individuals and their various enterprises, things start to blend together after a while, leaving us with the impression of having spent a day watching "the roaring and tumbling of waves in tempest" (EL2, 8). The highlights usually come in the form of wars (EL2, 9). Yet, "nothing is so barren as a soldier's brain. War," Emerson continues, "is one of those engrossing pursuits that like a passion for horses empties a man of all knowledge and all noble aims" (EL1, 255). "But what is the history of the remainder," Emerson wonders, "of the immense majority; of men and women who have not yet made their mark" (EL3, 86)? "To thought and freedom in individuals," Emerson concludes, "the whole system is hostile" (EL1, 255). Ordinary individuals appear in history as physical masses whose balance and distribution is shifted occasionally by the dynamics of great transactions, with the historical reports reading like "tables of a Life Assurance Company" (EL2, 8). "This is not History," Emerson concludes, "This is its shell from which the kernel is fallen" (EL2, 9).

The social obsession with material wealth and power discounts the cultural interest in the ordinary individuals. "Why are the masses, from the dawn of history down, food for knives and powder?" (W 4:30). "The cheapness of man," Emerson observes, "is every day's tragedy" (W 4:31). The corresponding traditional view of history, then, is premised on the fundamental insignificance of a powerless individual who has to be redeemed through *serving* the social structure or a greater cause, in the hopes of receiving some recognition in return for his service. The historical cultural representative function, then, is severed from the individual and transferred to the institution. Stripped of their natural dignity and self-respect "men do not imagine that they are anything more than fringes and tassels to the institutions into which they are born" (EL2, 218).

The point of an education in cultural history, on the contrary, is to "show you the riches of the poor . . . to show you that the common daylight is worth something" (LLR1, 354) – to learn the appreciation of a humble life. True, Emerson admits, "kingdom and lordship, power and estate, are a gaudier vocabulary than private John and Edward in a small house and common day's work; but the things of life are the same to both; the sum total of both is the same" (W 2:62–3). Royalty has so long "magnetized the eyes of nations" (W 2:63) that people tend to forget that the sovereignty they admire in kings is the privilege and right of every person who resolves to live her life in a sovereign fashion (W 2:63).

The material society, above all, desires stability (EL2, 197). It welcomes progress – when it comes to new technologies and new ways to increase its wealth – but the fundamental meaning-generating parameters of human existence must remain fixed: "natural" needs unquestioned, "self-evident" truths unmolested. It recommends, effectively, adapting to the prevailing established cultural framework instead of attempting to either transcend or transform it in significant ways. Its desire to retain its fundamental values as perennial, as rationally inevitable and naturally mandated, renders its orientation profoundly anti-historical, because history informs us that things must eventually change, the present will become the past, and the future may be very different from the present, condemning to obsolescence all the secure verities to which we cling. Because of this, ignorance of history and a cynical refusal to broaden one's horizons in the direction of cultural idealistic aspirations often go hand in hand. As Henry Adams noted concerning his and Emerson's contemporaries, the American mind "shunned, distrusted, disliked, the dangerous attraction of ideals, and stood alone in history for its ignorance of the past" (1918, 328).

This is not to deny of course, the importance of material resources as means of cultural progress. The point is, rather, that such progress can only be practically actualized within a concrete individual, who, in transcending her narrow individuality towards the more generalized possibilities of human nature, attains to a greater universality.[5] Hence, "all history exists for the Individual" (EL2, 173). And, by this measure, the material social advancement may often be of a marginal cultural significance: "the amelioration of outward circumstances will be the effect but can never be the means of mental and moral improvement" (W 1:281). Certainly, many people are much better off today – both mentally and morally – than they ever have been in the past; but our mental and cultural advancement is dramatically out of proportion to the immense material resources at our disposal. Ancient Greece could not conceivably match

[5] EL2, 14: "Progress belongs to individuals and consists in becoming universal."

the immense power of a modern society; but it could probably both match and even surpass it in terms of culturally significant productivity. Social and cultural progress may be related; but one does not automatically entail the other.

To conclude: On the one hand, the study of history performs for Emerson an indispensable role in the cultural self-formation. Its influence is both decentering and integrative insofar as history not only introduces a diversity of paradigms for forging a meaningful relationship with life under concrete circumstances, but also invites a reflective recollection that helps us to modulate and reconcile the apparently contrary tendencies in our character and thought. As Kateb explains, only surveying things retrospectively permits full play to the collisions of "contrasting or even directly opposed ideas and values, practices and institutions" (1994, 31). In the same vein, Emerson insists that "we cannot get far enough away from ourselves to integrate our scraps of thought and action, and to judge of our tendency and scope" (EL1, 225). The truth is, Emerson confesses, that in the end "we are unable to see our own life in perspective" (EL2, 16); and history, which enables us to see ourselves in and through others, provides the only remedy for this limitation (EL2, 16). Conversely, such sustained recollective historical reflection provides the only means for forming an adequate idea for how history itself should be written at present (EL3, 227).

No history is worth reading, according to Emerson, unless it is written with a "just estimate of human nature in mind" (EL2, 10). Without such a philosophically adjusted focus on the idea of humanity, history is liable to confuse the fundamental scales of significance, preserving tales of grand affairs of no intrinsic importance, while slighting the momentous moral and cultural developments unattended by pomp (EL1, 250). The narratives resulting from this misguided conception of history are written "for display" and are produced "after our own image and likeness, – three or four crude notions of our own, and very many crude notions of old historians hunted out and patched together without coherence or proportion" (EL3, 227). Emerson's kind of "philosophical" history, by contrast, would focus not on great deeds but art, religion, customs, language, nature, and above all, literature (EL1, 377 & EL2, 20). The general intention is to move away from the conventional political history (which often turns into "celebrity history") towards the history of the evolving methods of productive coping and learning, towards new strategies for expressing the intelligible content of lived human experience. This history is conceived, moreover, in a predominantly democratic spirit, meant to inspire artisans, doctors, and teachers rather than persons of eminence, conquerors, and dictators.

Still, may we not be entitled to expect more of history than Emerson is willing to provide? Collating the culturally significant possibilities of living, witnessing the distinctive operations of evolving social mechanisms refracted through the humanizing lens of the individual character: This modality of historical portraiture may provide us with important and ample materials for reflection, education, and even practical guidance. But then history as a discipline would dissolve into an intersection of essayistic literature and investigative journalism. As a discipline meant to generate its own distinctive forms of knowledge, history cannot restrict itself to the cataloging of cultural possibilities without inquiring whether some systematic patterns can be discerned in their genesis and interrelations. Many historians resist advancing things in this direction, equally wary of the conceptual pretensions of the speculative philosophies of history, and of the natural scientist's predilection for discovering regularities in the form of general law. Dewey, our next pragmatist figure, does not share these reservations: Systematic knowledge, in his opinion, can lead to the increase of functional control, which can prove essentially liberating when we contemplate our future in the light of the historical possibilities that we may want to perpetuate, develop, or bring about.

2 Dewey: Representative Situations and Historical Knowledge

2.1 History and Society

The pragmatist commitment to treating history as the preeminent source of insight with respect to the philosophical problem of self-knowledge foregrounds, simultaneously, its characteristic preoccupation with examining and fostering the diverse potentialities of the human nature. The fundamental plasticity of the human nature renders the distinction between its original unmodified constitution and the results of learning within a social environment decidedly elusive (LW.6.31 & LW.6.37 & LW.6.32). The "innate needs" of human beings, Dewey surmises, may not have changed much in the course of history (LW.13.286); however, their actual manifestations have varied stunningly across different cultural contexts (LW.13.287). The "importance of culture as a formative medium" (MW.14.230) as well the "immense diversities of culture" (LW.6.37) are so well recognized, in fact, that some caution to the contrary may be in order, lest we forget how enduring and tenacious the set patterns of "desire, belief, and purpose" can become (LW.13.291). Our analysis of human nature, as a consequence, needs to treat the natural and the cultural as the coordinate poles of an evolving dynamic relationship, rather than the fixed terms of a rigid dichotomy – a commitment reflected in Dewey's preferred phrases for his approach: "cultural naturalism" (LW.12.28) and "naturalistic humanism" (LW.1.10). What it aims to recognize and emphasize is the ineluctable interpenetration of physical and cultural heredity in the proper constitution of a human person (LW.12.49).

What distinguishes us from other animals is precisely the ability to preserve our past, to live in the world of things invested with complex meanings by previous human activities, "a word of signs and symbols" (MW.12.80), where most objects and events immediately portend more than their bare physical presence. If one wants to draw a line between nature and culture, it consists in the possession of history, which invests the natural world with fabricated meanings. In history also lies our freedom, because inherited meanings can be reinterpreted and reassigned, transforming the cultural world and the persons within it. Because of this, we can have education (as opposed to mere training) – a deliberate transformation or "modification of native human nature" resulting in the formation of new ways of thinking, desiring, and believing which bear little resemblance to our initial untutored inclinations (LW.13.292). Education, moreover, is seen by Dewey as a primary concrete point of application and testing ground for most historical-philosophical proposals concerning the constitution of human nature.

Culture, to paraphrase Thomas Alexander, is "the shared life of human beings upon the earth as it is appropriated in terms of [historically evolving] meaning and value" (1987, 71). So much of our thoughts, needs, aspirations, even reasoning powers, depend not on personal endowment and effort but on the general cultural background and instruction (MW.8.74). One could, in fact, say that "every culture has its own collective individuality" (LW.10.333). To participate in a culture, as Alexander notes, is to be able "to envision imaginatively, that is emotionally as well as conceptually, the ideals which integrate and determine the fundamentals" of its way of life (Alexander 1987, 271). Moreover, embracing an ideal requires conceiving of it as a promising possibility for actively restructuring our experience rather than merely assenting to an independently established truth (Alexander 1987, 256–7). Hence, living in a culture means also attempting to transform it.

The impulse to transformation, according to Dewey, usually begins with the individuals; but its influence remains severely restricted, unless it is incorporated into enduring structures and habits of the collective environment (MW.14.62). Changed personalities can only be created by social modifications (MW.12.192); suggesting, in turn, a rational obligation on the part of a growing society to remain especially attentive to the individual impulses, which can be utilized as agents of "steady reorganization of custom and institutions" (MW.14.72). "Invention is a peculiarly personal act" (LW.2.271), Dewey admits, but civilizational attainment of higher values must be a "mass achievement" and not "the work of a chosen few, of an élite" (LW.3.143). Here, one can grasp the principal contrast between Emerson and Dewey. Emerson is more interested in the tragic moment of expressive representative self-articulation, conceived of as an individual existential struggle; whereas Dewey is more concerned with the systematic development and social implementation of the melioristic structural possibilities suggested by such individual representative expressions. The individual insights, accomplishments, and revelations remain like so many plants in a herbarium unless taken up by a public.

Complex society, of course, consists of many interest groups, and the majority of individuals belong to several of them at once. The quality of the resulting public life depends directly on the capacity of these groups to interact productively and flexibly with each other. An esoteric cult or a robber band (to use Dewey's example; LW.2.328) exemplifies intrinsically closed social formations, meaning that their encounters with other groups will usually proceed in a confrontational modality. An intellectual discussion club, on the other hand, can serve as an example of an open and potentially interactive formation. Dewey welcomes the conflicts of interest and conflicts of perspective, even among the relatively closed outlooks. Customs and commitments – even when rigid and unintelligent in themselves – may be of good use simply because they "wear upon others," with frictions occasionally becoming a prelude to "liberations" (MW.14.90). In the more open settings, such confrontations can be staged as active deliberations: dramatic rehearsals of conflicting pertinent options and possibilities. "Variety of competing tendencies," argues Dewey, enlarges the world. It brings a diversity of considerations before the mind" (MW.14.137), helping us to uncover and articulate the full scope and nature of the conflicts between them.

Reasonableness is attained by learning to equilibrate between a variety of choices, interests, and values, instead of deciding on some unique set of the uniquely "correct" ones. Desirable happiness, a desirable life, according to Dewey, "is one that makes provision for continual enrichment of its own substance, and . . . this is impossible without continuous variation of its concrete aims" (MW.6.60). Hence, "desirable progress means, as a matter of fact, constant diversification," enabling the mind to "project new and more complex ends" (MW.10.45). How can the study of history contribute to this process of social growth and amelioration? One possible answer is that it can help us survey and clarify the multiform relationships between the aims posited as social ideals and the practical circumstances of their evolution and development.

As Alexander explains, Dewey's pragmatism "insists on understanding the actual in the light of the possible" (1987, 160), with the tension between the two establishing and preserving "the narrative, dramatic structure of existence" (1987, 52). The very idea of culture, according to Dewey, refers us to "the material and the ideal in their reciprocal interrelationships" (LW 1.363), to "a projection of what something existing may come to be" (LW.4.239). Ideals generally project "in securer and wider and fuller form some good which has been previously experienced in a precarious, accidental, fleeting way" (MW.14.20). The ideal, then, originates in the experience of the actual, which it consequently intends to elevate through a fuller realization of its own most promising potentialities. The shared imperative of all idealistic striving is growth. One serious trouble with the contemporary culture, therefore, is its tendency to regard individuals as "something given," already complete, with determinate fixed capacities and needs: "some thing whose pleasures are to be magnified and possessions multiplied" (MW.12.191).

Much of the common learning is motivated directly by economic utility, that is, "the ability of the learner to add to the earnings of others" (MW.10.45), while historical and social studies perform the auxiliary function of instilling the sense of "duties to the established order and a blind patriotism" (MW.10.148). In short, education is meant to shore up the actual, rather than to envision amendments to it in the name of an ideal. The truth, however, is that the established institutions and customs frequently fail to "correspond with the needs of our actual life" (Dewey 2012, 141), and require reform or abolition, so as to better serve the development of genuine human potentialities in the present.

The first condition for intelligent reform is the formation of the experimental attitude that has proved itself so fruitful in technology and science, yet meets with the most obstinate resistance when it comes to society and morals (LW.2.272). Instead of a purposeful rational reconstruction, the society's resistance is worn down by "an accumulation of stresses" (MW.14.73), with change eventually precipitated in response to a crisis. In such a society, ideals exist apart from reality – often to compensate the imagination for its narrowness and brutality (MW.10.48). The experimental attitude of a pragmatist, meanwhile, advocates a "practical idealism" (MW.10.48), wherein ideals become a concrete "collection of imagined possibilities that stimulates men to new efforts and realizations" (MW.12.147). However, for these projections to remain both realistic and practical, one must survey the past, focusing on the "peculiar types of social life; with the special significance of each and the particular contribution it has made to the whole world history" (MW.1.109). Only in this way can the old experience be "used to suggest aims and methods for developing a new and improved experience" (MW.12.133). The maintenance of this cultural continuity, which enables rational learning, is the function of historical literacy.

The possibility of cultural change often depends less on the concrete stimuli to action than on what Dewey calls "the climate of imagination" (LW.10.348). Because of this, the development of a "cultivated and effectively operative good judgment or taste" in the public provides for the most effective barrier against "the domination of belief by impulse, chance, blind habit and self-interest" (LW.4.209). Why is history well-positioned to play a leading role in the formation of cultural literacy and taste? The central philosophical problem for Dewey, as already mentioned, consists in the relationship "between the real and ideal," "between existence and value" (LW.1.310). In less abstract terms, this means finding ways for warranted beliefs "about the actual structure and processes of things" to interact effectively with the ideas that regulate human conduct (LW.4.15), to reconcile "the attitudes of practical science and contemplative esthetic appreciation," without which, we may become a pitiable "race of economic monsters" (MW.12.152). History naturally combines these two dimensions. Its narrative, dramatic (aesthetic) aspect frames its accounts of past social transformations in terms that refer to preferential valuation: success and failure, growth and decline, progress and tragedy; whereas its deliberately prosaic, evidential (scientific) side dispassionately details the structural conditions and variables, under which the value-driven forms of life have operated in the past and may well still operate (in some degree) to this day.

Does this not mean that we are bringing past history into the service of the present? It does. But, if history "be regarded as just the record of the past" (MW.1.104), as opposed to "a means of understanding the present" (LW.13.52), it becomes very difficult to see what its present significance might be. To ignore the past, Dewey argues, is "the sign of an undisciplined agent; but to isolate the past . . . is to substitute the reminiscence of old-age for effective intelligence" (MW.10.10). The forces and forms of social life change slowly; and even when entirely superseded (for the time being) can teach us something about the options and possibilities of human existence, and reasons and consequences entailed in the choices between them. Much of our conventional history still fails to record "the transitions and transformations of human activities" (MW.12.78–9), substituting instead "the political and chronological records that usually pass for history" (MW.1.15). Many conventional forms of historical narration (frequently revolving around the role of particular illustrious individuals) may not seem conducive to the social analytic function emphasized by Dewey. Still, there is no determinate obstacle to reconciling the different interests and modes of presentation, as long as a pragmatist interest in the possibilities of an intelligent transformation of historical human life receives recognition as one of our guiding considerations.

2.2 Hermeneutics of an Indeterminate Situation

The anchoring point of historical reflection is usually some kind of situation. Life, as Dewey suggests, "is a thing of histories, each with its own plot, its own inception and movement towards its close, each having its own particular rhythmic movement; each with its own unrepeated quality pervading it throughout" (LW.10.42–3). Once the experienced material "runs its course to fulfillment," we have what Dewey calls "an experience" – an experienced episode from which something can be learned (LW.10.42). The criteria of what serves as an appropriate experiential closure are basically aesthetic: A closure must be "consummating, not just terminating" (Hildebrand 2008, 158), with the sense of the episode's inner unity supplied by its "predominant mood" (LW.10.73).

The obvious implication is that the same sequence of events can be interpreted as several different situations – for example, as the destruction of the past or the birth of a new world – raising different questions and emphasizing different considerations. What is entailed in conceiving of something as a situation, ultimately, is the operation of "comprehension" – of "gathering together of details and particulars physically scattered into an experienced whole" (LW.10.60); with the resulting episode seen as salient enough to become at least "an object of narration in our ordinary conversation with others" (Dreon 2022, 73).

The situations that attract an historian's attention are generally drawn from the past transactions that form the subject matter of her research or from the history of the historiographical reflection thereupon. In one case, we are asking what compelled an agent to carry on in a certain way; in the other, what compelled an earlier historian to interpret the agent's actions in a specified fashion. The scope of an "historical" situation can vary widely in both cases: from a brief diplomatic altercation to the decline of an empire; from questioning the evidential basis of a transitory conclusion to disputing ideological bias in ascribing responsibility for a great war.

"The statement that individuals live in a world," says Dewey, "means, in the concrete, that they live in a series of situations" (LW.13.25). A situation is both individuated and made whole "in virtue of its immediately pervasive quality" (LW.12.73). The essential point to emphasize is that this overall quality, unlike the basic constituent elements of the situation, is genuinely unique (LW.12.74). All marriages are the same, in a way – with relatives, plans, and material possessions; yet, no two are the same in their experienced qualitative dimension, despite the common similarity of shared routines. Every marriage "feels" different and poses different problems. Sensitivity to this individuating quality is a cognitive virtue: It gives us an incipient sense of the pertinent relations in play and creates an intuitive resistance to the inappropriate imposition of habitual categories of analysis and judgment (LW.12.76).

A need for inquiry (or investigation) arises whenever we find ourselves in an *indeterminate situation* – one that gives rise to doubt (LW.12.3). There must be "something seriously the matter, some trouble" (MW.10.326) in order for us to "stop and think" (LW.1.237), to consider alternative possibilities. Only when our habitual ordinary ways of proceeding are impeded, do we consider reconceiving the situation analytically (Dreon 2022, 41).

Every situation "has its own organization of a direct, non-logical character" (MW.10.323). An indeterminate situation is one that is directly experienced as containing an objective conflict: The situation is an organized whole, yet one that is "falling to pieces in its parts" (MW.2.328). For example, we notice that the witness testimony somehow does not add up. In the course of a successful investigation, the initial conflict "loses vagueness and assumes more definite form" (MW.2.338). The resolution of a conflict results in a state of a newly attained equilibrium, enabling us to adopt a sustainable posture with respect to the situation as a whole.

The terms of an appropriate solution, however, can never be imposed. They must arise from the material in question, noting its previously ignored potentialities and imagining the possibilities they entail. The solution presents "old things in new relations" (LW.9.34), augmenting our understanding of the initial situation, and constituting a genuine episode of learning. Thus, questioning a witness' perceptual competence can significantly alter one's interpretation of the evidential landscape. A new perspective is tested "as glasses are tested; things are looked at through the medium of specific meanings to see if thereby they assume a more orderly and clearer aspect" (MW.1.161). But what one ends up seeing through these glasses is quite literally a new empirical situation, reconstructed with a view to a greater cognitive transparency (LW.4.70).

How does one secure an accomplishment of this sort? In the beginning, the meaning of some existential materials within a situation becomes spontaneously configured in the light of the interpreter's prior experience. "There is always something unquestioned in any problematic situation at any stage of its process" (MW.2.338), and so the first step is always to note "the constituents of a given situation which, as constituents, are settled" (LW.12.112). These become the "facts of the case," which "constitute the terms of the problem" (LW.12.113). This initial discernment of the meaning-bearing elements of the situation can be more or less promising: and its promise is assessed less with respect to its accuracy than its "directive power" in advancing the investigation (LW.12.512). It may be less important to remember the exact words of the witness' statement than to register an abrupt change in tone "at some point." The real probative value of various considerations and observations can only be assessed retrospectively, in the light of a resolved, intellectually reconstructed situation, and it would be unusual for the initial "state of facts" to remain unaltered "in respect to its content and its significance" at the end of a successful investigation (LW.12.145).

Little guidance is to be had beyond this schematic outline. The appropriate habits of interpretation are a matter of art – an ability formed through past experience (MW.14.48). Well-established habits generate ease in handling the appropriate subject matter but impede significant departures and narrow one's vision (LW.2.335). Flexible habits, sensitive to variations in the contexts of application result in a more refined perception and discrimination (MW.14.123). But the real question of "how" cannot receive a satisfactory answer because "even the most shrewd and successful man does not in any analytic and systematic way" know the system within which he operates or the skill that he deploys in navigating it (LW.2.338). The rules derived through methodological reflection on past successes are invaluable, but are limited and incapable, on their own, to generate a solution for complex and interesting cases.

So, what can be transferred from a successful solution of an historical puzzle to future inquiries, beyond some general methodological guidelines? The individual situation, Dewey reminds us, is unique; and so is the solution that restores its intelligibility (LW.12.523 & MW.8.45). Some general observations, perhaps? The use of generalizations in history is a contested matter because of the common theoretical emphasis on the individual nature of historical occurrences. Yet, unless one endorses some exuberant (and untenable) form of semantic holism, from claiming that no two individual situations are the same it does not follow that no aspect of two different situations can be regarded as the same in a practically pertinent sense. Here, we transition from the realm of historical hermeneutics to that of historical semiotics.

Objects are simply objects, and events are simply events. From a cognitive point of view, however, what matters about objects and events is their "representative character" (MW.4.95) – that is, their ability to serve as signs, as evidence (MW.6.109) – their significance and their meaning. Every element of a situation contains "potentialities which are not explicit; any object that is overt is charged with possible consequences that are hidden" (LW.1.28). Therefore, certain elements can always be read as signs, capable of reconfiguring the meaning of the situation as a whole. Thus, excessive enthusiasm from an ally may portend the possibility of betrayal, forcing us to reconsider what might "really" be going on in a diplomatic exchange.

The sign function is usually propelled to the fore whenever we find ourselves dealing with a perplexing, indeterminate situation, wherein our initial understanding or interpretation of things does quite add up. Puzzled, we begin to search for a clue, for some indication of what is actually at hand (LW.1.200). Similarly, a physician attempts to zero in on some telling symptom among her initial impressions: One that may suggest the right questions, the right procedures and tests, contributing to a gradual elaboration of a reasoned, evidentially grounded diagnosis (MW.10.340).

Our eventual reconstruction of what is "really" going on in a situation is never really "there" for us to apprehend – it is a product of *inference* – to be tested by subsequent observations. The betrayal is not an item concealed in somebody's pocket; we detect it as an intellectual construct, a hypothesis – the truth of which is known by the fruits that a real betrayal eventually bears. An inference always goes beyond the "assuredly present" (MW.8.71) to what is absent; because of this, it is capable of occasionally disclosing more than meets the eye. Because of this, also, its truth can only be corroborated by the test of some subsequent events or observations: It never simply corresponds to what already lies in plain sight: otherwise it would be a recording, not an inference. Because practical inference is of the nature of guessing, much of the technique of science (understood as a search for disciplined systematic knowledge) consists in finding "unambiguous, economical, and dependable signs" of forces and conditions incapable (under normal circumstances) of a more direct manifestation (MW.10.342). In fact, every research tradition can be seen as "an organized habit of vision" (LW.10.270), injecting most immediate and casual observations with "a complex apparatus of habits, of accepted meanings and techniques" (LW.1.170).

Stable and dependable signs have the logical form of a generalization. ("Hesitation is a sign of wavering loyalty.") Yet, such generalizations are not intended as universal laws; instead, they are instruments for a "better approximation to what is unique and unrepeatable" (LW.1.97). Their application in a specific situation is always a gamble and is always hypothetical (LW.4.132). Such general statements are, in fact, provisional abstractions, meaning that something has been isolated or released "from one experience for transfer to another" (MW.12.166). Abstraction is simply the most conventional device for applying the lessons of the preceding experiences to subsequent ones. If we abandon the habit of thinking about the resulting general statements as "a literal transcription of a general in existence" (LW.12.261), and think instead of their utility in advancing our investigations, then their role in explanation will be seen as enabling and liberating, rather than constraining. A mathematical circle is not fully matched by any existing figure (LW.12.303); yet, it is nearly indispensable in analyzing the logical possibilities entailed in some concrete arrangements. "A vision," Dewey explains, "is not a scene but it can enable us to construct scenes which would not exist without it" (LW.12.303).

2.3 History and Theory

History, according to Dewey, cannot be said to have emerged as long as it remains concerned with "isolated episodes" (LW.12.233); history requires an ordered temporal arrangement – a course of history. The historical character of an occurrence can only be disclosed as part of a succession of events forming a passage or a transition from one state of affairs to another (Dewey 2012, 222). Thus, history ultimately occupies itself with "strains of change" (LW.12.234), expressed through the sequentially ordered arrangements of carefully selected materials, bounded by the moments of initiation and closure.

Beyond the basic concern with factual accuracy, *science* distinguishes itself from the common sense by the predominance of the intellectual – as opposed to practical or institutional – interest (LW.12.56). The concepts and meanings of common sense are "coarse" (LW.12.56), aimed at utility and effective communication (LW.12.421). Science is less concerned with the "existential application," focusing instead on securing the "systematic relations of coherence and consistency" among its concepts (LW.12.71). This emphasis often leads to the formation of a "technical language" (LW.12.421).

History, at present, deliberately occupies an ambivalent territory: with much of the "ground-level" research conducted in increasingly technical terms, while the "higher-level" narratives most familiar to the general audience retain a principled loyalty to the common-sense idiom. Hence, the disparity between the different assessments of the scientific status of the field. On the side of the "controlled observations," the "collection of data and their confirmation as authentic" (LW.12.231), history conducts itself as a mature scientific discipline (consider the examples of epigraphy, paleography, numismatics, linguistics, bibliography), selecting its data rigorously on the basis of its evidential, inferential function (LW.12.232). Yet, on the side of the narrative, temporal order, there remains a pretense at a "natural" naïve perception – patiently recording the unfolding of the events as they are passing by. Temporal *quality*, argues Dewey, is "an immediate trait of every occurrence"; but temporal *order* "is a matter of science" (LW.1.92). It is a product of reflection, concerned to transform the meaning of the temporal sequence, so as to foreground the promising explanatory relationships. It is a product of an active judgment, not passive recording.

An event (an uprising, a quarrel) is "a term of judgment, not of existence apart from judgment" (LW.12.222). A judgment delimits the event, rendering it determinate and capable of entering into definitive relationships. It also inscribes it within a cycle of qualitative change that determines the subject-matter of a particular situation. (The beginning of a quarrel can be traced back to a childhood incident or a recent public encounter.) The historicizing operation is "necessarily selective," and the reasoning behind the selection is always supplied by some present interest (LW.12.234), including the anticipation of the future consequences of one's writing. Untimely meditations are liable to meet with unintended reception. At any rate, the judgment that institutes an event as a means of advancing a particular strand of historical understanding always positions it as a part of a larger course of historical events that the scrutiny of this event is meant to elucidate (LW.12.227).

Persons "occupied with management of practical affairs" have little use for such intellectual elaborations; to them all problems appear clearly defined in advance, with "the assumption that gross observation suffices to ascertain the nature of the trouble" (LW.12.487–8). Their diagnosis of the social conflicts assimilates them preferentially to "terms of moral blame and moral approbation"; a tendency that, on Dewey's view, presents "the greatest single obstacle" to the advancement of historical and social studies (LW.12.489). In every other domain, he ruefully observes, correctly framing the problem and proposing a tentative solution requires patient investigation; yet, in the social arena, having a "sure solution" formulated in advance passes for the sign of wisdom and authority (LW.12.490). However, without a disciplined scientific examination of conceptual alternatives, this mode of proceeding can only result in repeated partisan quarrels between "conservatives and progressives," "reactionaries," and "radicals" (LW.12.501).

Some voice, of course, a contrary concern: namely, that social science may displace the ideologically contested meanings by imposing a rigid uncompromising determinacy of its own, eliminating the productive exchanges between evolving alternative perspectives. Dewey dismisses this fear of a "final settlement" as practically and epistemologically unfounded (LW.12.42). The world is a process; and therefore, the future "although continuous with the past" cannot be "its bare repetition" (LW.12.46). New modes of interaction and comprehension must eventually arise, and new social problems come to dominate our intellectual horizons – forcing us, every time, to revisit our understanding of the past in a new light, and in connection with different interests, possibilities, and patterns of belief (LW.12.238). "History cannot escape its own process," Dewey argues, "It will, therefore, always be rewritten" (LW.12.238).

In fact, the qualities of "absoluteness" and "fixity" attach much more plausibly to the practical (rather than theoretical) contexts, where they are needed to secure the requisite confidence and "stability" of action (MW.1.157). A costly commitment cannot be sustained amidst the uncertainty regarding the meaning of its constituent causes and events: One must choose a side and put one's foot down. Similarly, when an historic occurrence (the assassination of Caesar) is mentioned as "an historic truth" rather than "an historic event," some moral, socially significant lesson must be intended rather than the mere "noting of an incident" (MW.6.13–4). Truth, in such cases, is primarily conceived of in terms of a social virtue, with its opposite being not error but a willful misleading of others (MW.6.14–15). To tell it "as it is" is to set the score straight, in a way that supports an account of the past that is congruent with our present practical motivation. It is about actively choosing to be "on the right side of history."

"In spite of the claims of ethical rigorists to the contrary," Dewey explains, "truth telling has always been a matter of adaptation to a social audience" (MW.6.15). Representing things correctly, in this context, does not simply coincide with forming an appropriate grasp of the object: One must also (and more importantly) conduct oneself in accordance with the appropriate social conventions. To misrepresent is not to simply claim something false – through blunder or ignorance – but "to distort and pervert" the conditions of discourse (MW.6.17). ("It is perverse to call our enemy's cruel actions *self-defense*.") Because of this – similar to a forgery – the more a distorted account resembles the truth, the worse it is (MW.6.17). With meaning thus conceived "in terms of social procedure and social consequences" (MW.6.21), a change in the social climate inevitably leads to the questions about "the nature and standard of truth" (MW.6.22).

What stands in the way of formulating a more sustainable conception of historical science is the misleading and mostly antiquated philosophical conception of knowledge as correspondence to reality. Applied to history, it convinces us that the proper aim of an historian is to produce a string of sentences or words that match the corresponding sequence of past events. This "spectator theory of knowledge," according to Dewey, is modeled on the idea of simply seeing things as they are (LW.4.19), the corollary being that an ideal representation of reality would be provided by a photographic fixation thereof. The trouble is that photographing things rarely, by itself, leads to an improved scientific understanding of them; and conversely, the most productive explanatory conceptions of modern science – for example, forces, charges, and fields – rarely designate something that can be literally seen. A pragmatist, moreover, does not generally begin with considering the possibility of knowledge in the abstract; instead, she starts with the best examples of knowledge that we have –

scientific knowledge, at present – and attempts to analyze them to discover the conditions of their perspicuous accomplishment (MW.13.59). Put together, these two observations do not bode very well for the correspondence theory unless its terms can be somehow reimagined.

Dewey proposes that, instead of conceiving of correspondence in terms of a duplication of reality by the mind, we interpret it in "the operational sense," wherein a theory or a description adequately answers (or corresponds to) the situation in the same way that a fitting response answers a question, or a key "answers the conditions imposed by a lock" (MW.14.179). To be in agreement with reality would mean to have such a conception of it as to be able to navigate it successfully by following one's resultant understanding. For an historian, this would mean the ability to cogently explain the meaning of the evidence already present at hand, and to anticipate the bearing of additional evidence that may be discovered, often aiding in its discovery. One tests a theory the way the glasses are tested: If things when looked through "the medium of specific meanings" assume a "more orderly and clearer aspect" (MW.1.161), then we have an incentive to pursue it further.

An operational conception of knowledge also has the advantage of avoiding the bizarre impression that the posits of our theory (economic cycles, dialectical tensions) designate some deeper, truer reality lurking underneath the apparent one – the ordinary reality that historical narratives typically describe. Dewey advocates a "naïve realism" with respect to ordinary human experience and practice (Hildebrand 2003, 26): Things are usually more or less what they seem, and what we thereby experience is about as real as it gets. Knowledge is a special modality of addressing and arranging our experience; and the objects of knowledge are the instruments and products of these special arrangements – not the "ultimately real" entities philosophers prefer them to be (LW.1.26). A scientific object is literally developed in the course of inquiry. We do not encounter electricity, for example, when we see a lighting. Instead, electricity is a complex explanatory construct, elaborated over hundreds of years, relating many phenomena (including the lightning) in a systematic fashion that admits of experimental verification and control. Eventually, we bundle our patterns of interaction with the electric phenomena into an impression of an entity capable of existing apart from its concrete manifestations. But that is merely a psychological fiction. Similarly, passing by the riots in the street one does not rub shoulders with the legitimation crisis; although, once the theoretical construct is in place, one can start clearly seeing signs and manifestations of a crisis on the street, among other places.

Scientific "objects" are instituted in the process of inventing appropriate concepts for intelligently ordering some related phenomena of interest. The object of knowledge is not something that an analysis begins with: It is the outcome of a successfully completed analysis (MW.10.368). Logically speaking, an object is "that set of connected distinctions or characteristics which emerges as a definite constituent of a resolved situation and is confirmed in the continuity of inquiry" (LW.12.513). We note certain interrelated characteristics of a political situation that form a causal nexus operating according to a more or less established pattern; we designate it as a certain type of "crisis" structure; we test and refine our model under a variety of circumstances; if it proves recurrently useful, people begin mentioning "crisis" on par with other real things that can be experienced, observed, etc. The acquired reality of a theoretical object – an object of knowledge – is well-earned, but it does not diminish or supersede the experienced reality of the concrete phenomena to which it relates and explains, nor does it prevent these phenomena from being subsumed as part of a different theoretical object: say, as "magnetic" rather than "electrical" phenomena, or part of a "reconstruction" process rather than a "crisis."

What is the aim of knowledge? Dewey claims that "we experience things as they really are apart from knowing"; whereas knowledge is a "mode of experiencing things which facilitates control" (LW.4.96), that removes difficulties and reduces uncertainty. Knowledge, moreover, results in an enriched conception of the object; it renders things "more richly meaningful" (Hickman 2007, 208) by disclosing their significant traits and potentialities (LW.1.285), permitting "new modes of interaction, having a new order of consequences" (LW.1.286). Knowledge, says Dewey, "is a mode of interaction; but it is a mode which renders other modes luminous, important, valuable, capable of direction" (LW.1.324). Common sense and hermeneutic understanding may enable us to sort out a particular situation; organized knowledge proposes to use the situation for the purpose of finding "indications of what will be experienced under different conditions" (MW.10.34). Knowledge emphasizes relations over isolated qualities (LW.12.119), ordering properties of interest according to their logical connections (LW.12.477), permitting free translation, inference, and "substitution of meanings" (LW.12.392), so as to expose the various interrelations between different situations, liberating a constellation of determining factors from the concrete but local situation, within which they are embedded. Theoretical objects (posits) are the vehicles of such transfer of meanings from one situation to another.

One could say that they are "real" or "true" if we construe "truth" in a pragmatist vein, as that which has gained an "an assured status" in the course of inquiry (MW.6.46), and can therefore be used as a secure "resource" in further investigations (Hildebrand 2003, 138). Under "novel and complex" conditions, however, such truths may be expected to undergo modification or revision (MW.6.47). Beyond this prosaic construal, in Dewey's opinion, there is not much to say about their reality since, on his pragmatist view, a discussion of reality "in general, überhaupt" is neither possible nor needed (MW.10.39). Philosophers tend to confuse themselves and others by referencing the "realities more real, more ultimate, than those which directly happen" (MW.10.39). Modern science, on the other hand, has taught as to regard our theoretical constructions as hypotheses (MW.4.100), with their truth attested to by the guidance they provide in conducting experimental observations and proposing robust explanations (MW.12.169). Whether we are right about the location of ancient Troy is determined by excavation; whether the document before us is "really" a forgery – by collecting additional evidence in the archives. How else can the truth be established, or its verification obtained, Dewey wonders: Do we "first look a long while at the facts and then a long time at the idea until by some magical process the degree and kind of their agreement become visible?" (MW.4.85).

We must set aside the idea of knowledge as the relationship between the mind and the world and focus instead on the "connections that are found among known events" (Dewey 2012, 182). As historians, we must give up on the philosophical problem of getting in (present) touch with the (absent) past and focus on the way in which patterns of human interaction are altered under variable conditions. "Relative invariants" may play an important role in this enterprise, but only as mechanisms, as "relations between changes, not the constituents of a higher realm of Being" (LW.4.67). Facts certainly have a decisive role to play; but being a fact is not determined merely by being "real."

Events in themselves are not facts; and many events, while real, are perfectly irrelevant. To call something a "fact" is to accord it a special *authority*, "to determine belief and decide the conclusion to be reached in a given field of subject matter" (Dewey 2012, 138). Facts are carefully selected from the panoply of existentially available materials based on their "probable evidential significance" (LW.12.130) for the problem at hand; and it requires great skill to decide "what can safely be taken as there, as given in any particular inquiry" (MW.2.347).

To produce the iron that is used in research and manufacture from iron found in its natural form, Dewey argues, required a great art; and similarly, the way that "the things of our primary experience are resolved into unquestioned and irreducible data" requires great art and technique developed over generations (MW.10.345). Our simplest, most unequivocal data are a product of great contrivance.

The contrary belief, that the data of research are to be provided by "direct and uncontrolled experience," had been one of the principal obstacles overcome by the scientific revolution (LW.4.206). As long as this view was endorsed, explanation consisted simply in bringing the "naively experienced material" under some logical form (LW.4.71), resulting in "an artistic whole for the eye of the soul to behold" (LW.4.73). This corresponds closely to the still current notion that the writing of history consists in subjecting the recorded facts to some form of dramatic narrative emplotment. In fact, Dewey cites this as a problem of social inquiry in general: namely, that its materials exist "chiefly in a crude qualitative state" (LW.12.487).

Every object or event that offers itself to our attention "extends beyond itself" (MW.8.91) because it is embedded in the larger world. Hence, we cannot be said to possess an adequate understanding of an event (say, a coronation in Rheims) unless we understand what its occurrence entails and what it would entail, had the circumstances been different. (There are, of course, many well-ascertained events in history that we do not sufficiently understand.) The significant traits of an event are pregnant with consequences and, because of this, they can perform a "diagnostic" function (LW.12.269), serve as signs capable of entering into chains of conjecture and evidential reasoning.

The natural objects of scientific study, such as iron or clay, acquire new meanings and new potentialities, and come to stand now for many things to which they once were thought to have no determinate connection (LW.12.132). Could not a similar development obtain in the case of some historical character types, situations, and transaction mechanisms? It is probably impossible to build our understanding of the past exclusively around the phenomena and entities that admit of such conceptual growth and elaboration. Nevertheless, to the extent that such conceptually differentiated materials can serve as "levers" for advancing the progress of concrete investigations (LW.12.382), suggesting logical connections and possibilities worth pursuing or eliminating, their importance for the prospects of a systematic disciplined inquiry cannot be ignored. In fact, Dewey is convinced that "the problem of institution of methods by which the material of existential situations may be converted into the prepared materials which facilitate and control inquiry is . . . the primary and urgent problem of social inquiry" (LW.12.487).

All of this need not sound esoteric: Many of the terms that we use routinely as a matter of course are, historically, products of prior theoretical conjectures and careful research (LW.12.122). We see cuneiform, for example, and spontaneously append to it a complex constellation of images and meanings that would simply be unavailable to an untutored observer. But the concept and its implication have become so standardized and familiar that we may be liable to confuse its routine descriptive employment with a common-sense perceptual report.

The cognitive purpose behind the development of reliable theoretical posits and the progressive institution of the refined or "prepared" data is the same: to facilitate the process of secure, responsible inference. Intelligence consists of the ability to regard things "in their capacity of signs of other things" (LW.4.170). Detecting an ally's hesitation is a matter of focused attentiveness; interpreting (or inferring) its significance for the progress of a negotiation is a matter of intelligence in the relevant sense. We are interested in the characteristic properties of objects and events in their capacity as "potentialities" (LW.4.110) that may yield distinctive sets of significant results under different conditions. A prediction also serves as a criterion of an adequate understanding: The ability to explain the particular outcome of a negotiation is related to the ability to offer predictions about what would have happened had the enabling conditions been altered in pertinent ways.

Once again, the aim of developing theoretical models, posits, and procedures is not to establish their own uncontested reality (in the manner of a covering law) but to provide useful instruments for the advancement of research. Hence, the "discovery of difficulties," "noting apparent exceptions, negative instances, extreme cases, anomalies" plays an essential role in the pragmatist picture (MW.1.169): It is in the nature of instruments to be improved, adjusted, or even discarded in the light of the changing purposes. Such constructivist nonchalance may produce some well-justified anxiety among serious historians who are concerned, after all, to describe, explain, and understand very real events and situations – not engage in stimulatingly artful experimentation with conceptual scaffolding. Where, in this account, does one find the historical reality, understood in the ordinary practical – not esoteric, philosophical – sense?

Dewey's basic answer is that we find it in the well-understood, clarified situation that emerges once the research problems are solved. The main point of a theoretical analysis is to produce "a new object of experience," which confers a new "depth, range and fullness of meaning" upon the initial, naively experienced circumstances (LW.4.152). When a muddled but violent affair resolves itself, on the basis of carefully examined evidence, into a virtually incontestable failed murder plot, we have touched potentially on something both real and enduring. Laws and rules, argues Dewey, are merely "intellectual instrumentalities" that assist us in determining the meaning of the case (LW.4.164): The "full and eventual reality of knowledge is carried in the individual case, not in general laws isolated from use in giving an individual case its meaning" (LW.4.166). This is why concrete findings and paradigmatic results in science survive so easily the challenges and revisions to the theoretical frameworks that generated them. If a Marxist analysis enables us to comprehend more fully and accurately the complex of relationships involved in a specific industrial transformation, by bringing to light new problems, new evidence, and new relations, then we are entitled to retain our enriched understanding of the individual situation, even as we question the theoretical principles employed to attain it. A converse procedure of adjusting our understanding of concrete historical situations to support or fit some cherished set of theoretical premises constitutes a flagrant (but regrettably common) abuse of history.

2.4 Conclusion

At present, history remains significantly undertheorized, in part due, undoubtedly, to the reluctance often felt at the prospect of admitting the "technical," experimental attitude of modern science into the domain of traditional moral judgment, or the so-called "human concern." We live in a world where scientific procedures are less trusted than political allegiances. Yet, before we succumb to the usual anxieties about science's cold deterministic authority, we may briefly consider Dewey's warning that a scientific attitude is also a means of "emancipating us from enslavement to customary ends, the ends established in the past" (MW.8.81), conducive to the development of new, untried possibilities of experience (MW.1.170). History, which refuses on principle to conduct itself as a science, may become ensnared instead by conventional loyalties and political interests. If we believe that scientific reason may displace our old traditional values, we must trust it also to assist in the creation of new ones (LW.13.172).

During "the greater part of the history of European thought," Dewey observes, the prevailing conceptions of the explanatory mechanisms of human nature simply reflected and supported the needs of the "practical social movements" (LW.6.37). Social tendencies "are read back into the structure of human nature; and are then used to explain the very things from which they are deduced (LW.13.139). Human nature is believed to be moved by an "inherent love of freedom" in the time of political reform, and by self-interest and profit in the time of industrial and mercantile development (LW.13.75). Historical psychology, in this wise, simply becomes a "branch of political doctrine" (LW.13.84). Existing modes of social behavior are first converted "into a psychological property of human nature," and then into a "principle of value – a moral matter" (LW.13.147). Under an intellectual regime of this sort, the explanatory power remains ephemeral, because the explanation simply feeds the audience its own prejudices masquerading as insights, and systematic consistency becomes virtually impossible, because each new social fashion brings with it a newly favored set of foundational explanatory terms.

If history is to serve the interests of education and intellectual growth – instead of the transient political interests – it must exercise systematic care to elicit the genuine "representative function" of different patterns of interaction with the "socio-cultural conditions" (Dewey 2012, 189). A representative character, transaction, or situation project onto the world a certain constellation of ordering structures, exposing common mechanisms, disclosing novel objective possibilities, and sustainable forms of transition between different modalities of engagement with the shared world. What renders some cases "representative," constituting the proper "specimens" of a determinate kind (LW.12.432)? What renders the *Donation of Constantine* a paradigmatic example of historical forgery? Or Brutus a canonical rebel?

Questions of this sort cannot be answered by collecting similar cases and abstracting their common properties (LW.12.429). An artless survey – however extensive – does not permit one, usually, to distinguish between the ubiquitous superficial resemblances and important constitutive analogies; resulting frequently in an arbitrary suppression of relevant differences and atypical cases. Even a fair statistically representative sample does not usually answer the need for a genuinely representative *exemplary specimen*: An average student need not illustrate the defining characteristics of studenthood. In fact, the common notions of statistical representative generalization may prove substantially misleading with respect to the problem of representation conceived in the pragmatist vein.

A genuine specimen, in Dewey's intended sense, permits one to draw secure inferences about (as yet) unobserved traits of the situation on the basis of certain observed constitutive characteristics (LW.12.474). If a document is an anachronistic forgery of a certain sort, then we can expect certain types of irregularities to emerge on closer inspection, in addition to the ones that had prompted our suspicion in the first place. If an insurgency rightly falls under a certain category, then it will not be followed by an attempt to establish a new dynastic rule.

We compare the subsequent cases to the specimens constituted as exemplary, in virtue of a characteristic "order of interactions or of functional correlations of variations" (LW.12.435); and only in cases where the right "ordered set of cojoined traits" is discovered (LW.12.474), do we feel entitled to resort to appropriately qualified generalizations. The ground of the generalization, in science as well as in history, for Dewey, is a "coherent individualized situation" (LW.12.450), with the interrelations of its constituent elements understood well enough for it to serve as a model or a diagram for examining the individual composition of sufficiently analogous situations. The generalization, in this case, proceeds by means of a disciplined systematic comparison.

When this care and discipline are neglected, we begin to treat the theoretical objects of historical experience as "natural," obviating the history of their artefactual derivation and construction, diminishing thereby our propensity to become reflexive about the appropriateness of their prospective employment. We assume that the new situations we encounter are sufficiently similar to the former ones, that the terms and the outcomes of the prior conceptual analysis can be carried over without modification. We continue to use the same concepts – say, *democracy* – to describe very different political formations, with the false continuity occasionally suggesting misleading ideological implications.

The historical, social world and the principles and mechanisms, on the basis of which its operations can be rendered intelligible, change; therefore, our conceptual instruments must be undergoing not only refinement but also a recurrent "vital readaptation" (MW.14.165); and this requires both precision in use and a constant awareness that their meaning is produced and developed in specific historic and analytic contexts and is not in any sense neutrally or naturally given.

This does not imply, moreover, that the theoretically elaborate concepts and their objects can claim some sort of existential primacy over the words and objects of common experience; nor that they can be unproblematically substituted for each other in the course of ordinary practice. A thermometer cannot substitute for a fever, however useful it may prove (diagnostically) in selecting an appropriate remedy. The cognitive advantage of theoretically constructed objects derives entirely from the logical function they are capable of performing in the course of a disciplined inquiry; in that sense, their primary distinction from ordinary everyday things is indeed primarily a matter of a "logical form" (Hickman 2007, 213).

To sum up: On the view presented thus far, the classical pragmatist tradition, spanning Emerson and Dewey, was centrally preoccupied (among other things) with the notion of representation as *representativeness*; according it a significant and prominent role in the study of history, with a view to understanding the emergent transformative potentialities of the historically conditioned development of human character. Meanwhile, a large proportion of historians as well as twentieth-century philosophers have been attracted to a very different conception of representation: namely, representation as correspondence to an untheorized reality – to things "as they actually are" – or, in the case of history, "once were." Pragmatists, as we have seen in the case of Dewey, consider this notion of representation both untenable and misleading. In fact, the vigorous reentry of pragmatism into the central philosophical debates at the close of the twentieth century is frequently (and rightly) associated with

Rorty's influential critique of the conventional representational paradigm across disciplines, clearing the conceptual space for a return to the pragmatist concern with cultural-historical representation in the context of a contemporary democratic society.

3 Richard Rorty's Critique of Representational Correspondence

3.1 Reality and Truth

It is commonly believed that Rorty may have had something important to communicate to historians about reality and truth. In fact, what he would have probably said is that historians need not worry about the philosopher's notions of reality and truth, and should feel free to define both (or either) in any way that accords best with their historical purposes. We do not call upon a linguist to have a conversation, nor upon a chemist to select the ingredients for a pie. Whence, then, the ubiquitous need for a philosopher's narrow expertise?

In other words, it must be entirely possible to make warranted historical statements about truth without having an underlying *philosophical* theory about truth, or even implicitly presupposing one; and the same, pretty much, goes for "reality." To attest plainly to the reality of a chair that one is sitting on does not require answering odd questions about what the reality of a chair consists in, or how one can ascertain its genuine participation in true reality. These are, of course, philosophical questions. For a philosopher, the pertinent conception of "true reality" performs the function of postulating, underneath the apparent diversity of experienced appearances, an underlying rationally coherent unity that thought alone can grasp.

According to Rorty, this way of conceiving the world can be traced all the way back to Parmenides who was the first (in the West) to roll up the entirety of being into a "well-rounded blob" (Rorty 2016, 2). Wherefore this interest in Unity? The Western culture, Rorty explains, was searching for "a set of beliefs that would end, once and for all, the process of reflection on what to do with ourselves" (2010a, 475). The notion of a true reality was meant to fulfill the resulting need "to fit everything – every thing, person, event, idea, and poem, into a *single context*, a context that will somehow reveal itself as natural, destined and unique" (2007, 90).[6] When everything is placed in its true relationship to everything else, reason is placed in the position to pronounce its final judgment.

[6] Italics added for emphasis.

To grasp this philosophical conception of reality, you cannot orient yourself to the mundane "endorsement of such things as rain and bears," you must instead try to conceive of "something august and remote"; in fact, the best way to get a proper feel for this reality is to "become and epistemological skeptic" – wondering whether such a sublime thing could ever come within our human grasp (Rorty 2021, 2–3). Hence, ever since Plato, "there have been people who worried about whether we can gain access to Reality, or whether the finitude of our cognitive faculties makes such access impossible" (Rorty 2007, 105).

Rorty, for his part, claims that "truth and reality exist for our social practices rather than vice versa" (2007, 7). Far from signifying an *external destination*, towards which our conversations are perpetually striving to progress, both abbreviate a certain growing complex of critical operations *within* our discourse, wherein they originate. To learn what it means to say "true" of a witness report, on this view, is not very different from learning how to decide that a bicycle is in a "good condition." We begin with discussions about the relative success of our social practices, and eventually learn to introduce certain helpful distinctions and rules to facilitate their functioning.

Understanding what truth is, then, requires no more than a (usually implicit) grasp of the way that "true" functions in the speech of a competent interlocutor. As practically and socially apt creatures, we are simply entitled to define "true" and "real" in terms of the "language I know" (Rorty 1988, 222). We recognize things as true because they sound true in our language, and – within our language – we, the competent speakers, are quite good at discriminating between the appropriate and the inappropriate uses of "true." We cannot get to a sense of truth deeper than the full sense of "true" that is implicit in the current cultural phase of our linguistic competence.

This, however, begs the question of whether our language itself is adequate to reality, and whether it latches onto it in the right way. Rorty's cleverly phrased rejoinder is that "asking how languages manage to represent reality seems a bit like asking how it is possible for wrenches to wrench" (1992, 370). Language, he argues, must be construed in a Darwinian vein, not as something apart from reality – trying to ape it the best it can – but as an evolving system that "simply abbreviates our various complex interactions with the universe" (Rorty 2021, 98). Insofar as we – the essentially languaged beings – remain apt and practically grounded in our everyday world, our language cannot fail to remain substantially adequate, in turn: for to have a world or reality, in our case, must itself be understood fundamentally as a function of linguistic representation.

To become a competent language-user means to already know enough about reality and truth in order to get around. Yet, behavior becomes "properly linguistic only when organisms start using a *semantical metalanguage* and become capable of putting words in intensional contexts" (Rorty 2021, 99), – that is, when they start reflexively commenting on the appropriateness of deliberate word use, saying things like "This may seems like an X, but actually it is not." "True" and "real" are two cardinal items belonging to the semantic metalanguage that enables us to "comment on and criticize our overt verbal performances" (Rorty 2021, 162). The development and articulation of the pertinent norms governing their use require great lengths of cultural time and considerable intellectual sophistication. Nevertheless, the resulting normative constraint, to cite Brandom, is "wholly our creature, a historically sedimented accumulation that is instituted by our own social practices" (Brandom 2021, xii) – an advanced instrument of thought rather than something that exists either prior to or apart from it.

For a pragmatist, then, designating something as "real" or "true" corresponds to assigning it a certain important (but revisable) role within our thinking: as a ground for further inferences, as something against which other candidate truth-claims must be measured, etc. Consequently, the other philosophical question – of what "true" and "real" might mean entirely apart from our thought – is regarded by them as irrelevant and unproductive.

If we are concerned with truth in the ordinary sense, this analysis has little bearing on its fortunes. In fact, Rorty repeatedly emphasized that he had no objections to the "homely and shopworn" conceptions of reality and truth (1979, 307), to the "un-exciting notion of true" that appears in concrete, situated inquiries.[7] The target of his criticism was truth in the "special philosophical sense" (Rorty 1979, 307) adumbrated above. The truth of our ordinary beliefs about the experienced world, pace Rorty, is much clearer conceptually than the nebulous notion of things as they are "in themselves" (2021, 3). Sadly, he writes, whenever people "step outside of their expert cultures – when they stop acting as carpenters or physicists and start getting reflective in religious or philosophical ways – they do, alas, start wondering about whether we are shadowing, displaying, mirroring, and representing something. I wish they did not" (Rorty 1995, 195). In the end, "there is nothing to be said about either truth or rationality apart from descriptions of the familiar procedures of justification" (Rorty 1990, 23) employed by our peers in a social or professional practice. Any attempts to "ground a practice on something outside the practice will always be more or less disingenuous" (1996, 333).

In other words, we can and must have productive arguments about truth in specific contexts, as long as we concede – at the meta-level – that truth is not

[7] Cf. Voparil 2022, 73.

something "one should expect to have a philosophically interesting theory about" (Rorty 1982, xiii), something that calls for or repays a systematic philosophical analysis (1989, 9). It is no more necessary to have a philosophical theory about the nature of truth, Rorty intimates, than to have one about the nature of danger (Rorty 2021, 52): All we need are some tolerably reliable ways of detecting and responding to either one. If there is to be some general, philosophical conception of truth it had better be a *fallibilist* one: one that employs "true" in a cautionary sense to flag "a special sort of danger" (Rorty 2021).

Sometimes we believe ourselves to be entirely justified, beyond reasonable doubt, in convictions that later turn out to be demonstrably false. To account for the possibility of such relative ignorance in comparison to somebody in possession of a wider relevant epistemic context (Rorty 1979, 292), we may want to include a disclaimer in declaring our position: stating that, although at present we feel perfectly justified in adhering to it, with no known outstanding objections or qualifications, there could be – in *truth* – something more to the matter at hand, although currently this possibility itself remains purely conjectural. Rorty glosses this point by suggesting that, perhaps, instead of "truth," we could capture this fallibilist concern by distinguishing between the "present and future justifiability" (Rorty 2021, 53).

But what if the future justification practices turn out to be as parochial and misleading as our own? The traditional conception of truth had the merit of confronting this possibility with a standard independent of all prevailing opinions. Rorty does concede that it would be nice to have such a standard, as long as we could be sure that we have the right one. The problem, Rorty explains, is that "you cannot aim at something . . . unless you can recognize it once you've got it" (2021, 48). We can often recognize greater integrity, greater patience, and greater charity (2021, 57); we can recognize a secured agreement or a dissipated doubt (2021, 136); but we do not know how to tell a truth from a lie just by staring it in the face. Philosophers have repeatedly attempted to address this problem by trying to articulate "a general theory of representation" (Rorty 1979, 3) rooted in the correct exercise of special mental processes (Rorty 1979, 6), meant to constitute reason and rationality. The exercise of reason, on this view, enables us to discern the "really real" (Rorty 2007, 78) among the apparently persuasive, yet potentially deceptive, conceptual possibilities.

Rorty counters this proposal with the observation that *reason* is not to be found in an individual mind: instead, it is an artifact of historical social practice. Rationality, he insists, "is a social phenomenon, not one that a human organism can exhibit by itself" (Rorty 2007, 176). Examining the hardware of a computer cannot enable us to deduce the logic of its variegated external uses and applications (Rorty 2007, 179). Similarly, examining the structure of the individual mind can only shed a limited light on the complex cultural practices, including practices of inquiry or research. What renders our mental functioning reasonable, Rorty argues, is not a set of privileged psychological operations but, rather, the internalized external norms (or rules) (Rorty 2007, 179) that discipline them into various organized regimes of operation.

The study of the history of culture is the study of the emergence and development of these norms in the course of their gradual implementation. It is a genealogical story of the intellectual transformations that help us explain how the cave dwellers who painted animals on the walls have eventually become ourselves, with our intricately derived ideas and institutions. This social, cultural history is the only true history of reason, comprehended in its social essence. In retracing it, we learn an important lesson: namely, that "objective criteria do not drop down from heaven but are themselves historical products" (Rorty 2016, 49). Hence, we have many useful, evolving epistemic rules and principles of variable scope and intent; but no one universal rule, such as "do not stray far from the sense data," "cleave to clear and distinct ideas," or "mind the representational correspondence."

This social, cultural conception of reason effectively forestalls any possibility of an a priori conceptual shortcut towards a conclusive formulation of the universal conditions of ideal representation – the criteria of the "really real."

Another common source of the misplaced desire for the ultimate reality transcending our ordinary conceptions relates to the intellectual influence of natural science. The advance of the natural sciences, coinciding with the advent of modernity, had done much to undermine the conventional notions of accurate representation. New modes of analysis – unexpected, experimental, unapologetically abstract – offered little solace to the "realistic" intuitions of common sense. The previously "natural" modes of understanding the physical world were shown to be shallow and, ultimately, misleading.

As Robert Brandom explains, the "premodern philosophical tradition understood the relations between mind and world, appearance and reality, in terms of *resemblance*" (2021, xiii). Starting with Descartes, at least, this naïve conception of representation becomes fundamentally untenable: Things turn out to be very different from what they seem, even upon most attentive observation. The common-sense view essentially presupposed a mirroring relationship between an accurate representation and its object. One represents an orange by a careful realistic drawing; a conversation, by a meticulous transcript – with the degree of correspondence established by comparison to the original. The new scientific dispensation, on the other hand, informs us that quadratic equation corresponds to a parabola despite the total absence of a resemblance between the two.

Parabola is *essentially* a quadratic function: What matters are no longer the appearances, but the underlying structural configurations, the theoretical "mechanisms."

Essentialist strategies are also common in historical practice. An interest in offering a total, comprehensive account of immensely complex social developments has often prompted theorists to focus on some "essential" or "predominant" factor (De Certeau, 120) as a key to what genuinely matters. Such approaches have their uses; however, an historical process is not a fixed substance, whose essential character can be captured by a semblance of a chemical formula. As Rorty explains, societies, countries, and historical entities of various sorts have *histories* but do not have *natures* (Rorty 2022, 175). These histories can be narrated in many different ways, with many different intentions and uses. But none of them can lay a legitimate claim to grasping the *essential* nature of an historical subject or a period, or to claim precedence on the basis of a perceived proximity to any such essentialist comprehension: The reason being simply that it is not possible to get closer to something that is not there to begin with.

Rorty's own anti-essentialism is rooted in his commitment to *relationalism*: The idea that everything is "what it is by virtue of its relations to everything else," and all such relations "are in constant flux" (Rorty 2007,128). The meaning of words in a language affords one example of such relational determination; another example is numbers. We cannot be essentialist about numbers because all there is to a number is its relation to other numbers; and Rorty proposes extending this relationalist conception to other things – "there is nothing to be known about them except an infinitely large, and forever expansible, web of relations to other objects" (Rorty 2021, 88). Our concrete and definitive statements about the properties of particular entities, processes, and events are merely ways of "spotlighting certain webs of relationships rather than other webs" (Rorty 2021, 86).

Economic relationships can be highlighted at the expense of geo-political ones; a cultural or philosophical dimension of an historical formation can occasionally exceed its economic and political significance, or be regarded as virtually negligible in comparison. Different contexts accord priorities to different types of relationships. The reason that some of these end up being regarded as essential or central in particular instances stems from the fact that some contexts and considerations have become very obvious and familiar, whereas others remain comparatively unexplored and are, therefore, regarded as optional or even marginal (Rorty 2021, 91). But this relative ordering of contexts is itself a product of history and is subject to historical change. There is, moreover, no such thing as the ultimate, final context; although this contention itself is a matter of pragmatist faith, with which Rorty invests the Emersonian "prophecy" that every context is eventually bound to be superseded by another, larger one (Rorty 2016, 40).

In conclusion, pragmatists disown the traditional metaphysical conceptions of reality and truth by embracing a mundane conception of historically developing rationality; a relational, culturally informed conception of reality; and an inferential conception of truth grounded in successful social practices. Consequently, they reject the idea of a uniquely correct representation of reality underwritten by the claims of a privileged correspondence. Many different representations, reflective of different interests and possessed of different virtues, can be said to be substantially in accord with reality, without laying claim to unconditional precedence. There is no one true History, no complete or essential historical context. Still, perhaps a more modest conception of representational correspondence could prove itself useful in grounding a warranted sense of historical realism.

3.2 Representation as Correspondence

Rorty's overt intention is to relinquish the epistemological significance accorded to the notion of representation altogether, to give up on the idea of "matching" our narratives, theories, and statements to reality. Having rejected the traditional essentialist and reductionist strategies for reasons adumbrated above, he proceeds to admonish his audience against the general temptation to postulate some determinate content or structure underneath the apparent indeterminateness of our ordinary experience (Rorty 2014, 35). We can produce accounts of reality serving different interests and purposes with greater or lesser success; but reality, on its own, does not contain an originary account of itself: "The world is out there, but descriptions of the world are not. Only descriptions of the world can be true or false. The world on its own – unaided by the describing activities of human beings – cannot" (Rorty 1989, 5).

The world can influence our judgments and beliefs, but this does not mean that "the world splits itself up, on its own initiative, into sentence-shaped chunks called 'facts'" (Rorty 1989). Therefore, the decision to use a particular vocabulary or a description must involve a selection, a choice. Language cannot passively record; even in the most prosaic reporting, it must always introduce an element of active comprehension, reconfiguring its pronouncements in the light of some relevant space of intelligible relationships.

However, even if we follow Rorty in giving up on the "notion of language as fitting the world" (Rorty 1989, 28), we may still be drawn to the idea of some form of answerability obtaining between the actual state of affairs and our accounts thereof. Granting that we cannot objectively *discern* the outlines of our stories and theories in the world, cannot obtain a neutral transcript of the intended plot and animating mechanism, might we not, nevertheless, *compare* our stories and theories to the outcomes of our transactions with the world: The way we compare a statement about the contents of a box with what is discovered once the box is open?

This paradigm, in Rorty's opinion, may function rather well in the case of isolated descriptive statements that appear to ground our correspondence intuitions in seemingly unproblematic ways. A statement, "the tomato is on the table" is easily verified by examining the plausible table-candidates in our vicinity for the evidence of tomato-resembling objects. The real problems with correspondence arise in connection with conflicting high-level narratives or theories that tend to postulate complex, non-observable relationships and mechanisms. For example, whether a series of historical transitions is best explained by the changing conceptions of freedom or by the evolving relationships of production is not a question that can be easily settled by examining the corresponding "realities." The posits of such theories are not derived in any straightforward manner from verifiable observations and are often roughly compatible with much of the same historical evidence.

If we cannot match theories to reality element-by-element, or statement-by-statement, correspondence itself must be construed as a holistic relationship: either the shoe fits or not; and there is no way to tell for certain, in advance of trying it on. Since there is no such thing as a perfect fit, different conflicting theories or stories may fit "more-or-less" for somewhat different reasons and in somewhat different ways. So, instead of comparing theories to reality, we begin comparing our theories to competing theories. However, there appears to be no neutral ground on which to compare them: because reality itself is ostensibly incapable of providing a theory of its own.

As Rorty puts it, we have no idea "what it would mean for Nature to feel that our conversations of representation are becoming more like her own" (Rorty 1979, 299). Therefore, we can never completely step outside of our own theoretically inflected languages, to render an impartial judgment regarding the goodness of fit between the competing candidate descriptions and the world that they purport to represent.

With history, things tend to be somewhat different because, within its purview, we are frequently accountable to others – the historical agents, their descendants, or past historians – who describe the same events and describe themselves in significantly different ways. In Rorty's view, this is, in fact, part of the solution to the problem: justifying our descriptions to others who may disagree with them must be the focus of our cognitive efforts, rather than holding ourselves answerable to an uninterpreted reality, posited as a criterion of objective neutrality. It is precisely in the context of our exchanges with others that comparing "language games" or "vocabularies as wholes" (Rorty 1989, 5) acquires its critical bite: All we need to concede is that such conversational, social comparisons can and must replace the earlier outdated conversations about correspondence.

The fact that reality cannot serve as a *normative criterion* in making these comparisons – cannot lay down the rules to govern the selection and evaluation of the promising candidates – should not be interpreted to mean that reality imposes no constraints on this process. It is just that these constraints are of a *causal*, not a normative, sort. Sometimes our theoretical proposals run head-first into a seemingly impenetrable wall: When their core predictions fail, for example, or new evidence confounds their core expectations. They can also suffer gradual attrition over time, with a series of explanatory difficulties, and availability of alternative options, eventually diminishing their perceived worth to marginal or negligible. Finally, some theories continue to fare exceptionally well, even though there are good reasons to suspect their cardinal posits. In each case, we are entitled to state that "reality" has been resistant to the theory or has favored its advance; but the reasons why cannot be stated in a similarly uncontroversial manner – they are subject to potentially controversial interpretations.

Reality exercises a pressure on action and thought. What shows us that "life is not just a dream" is precisely this causal, "non-intentional, nonrepresentational" pressure (Rorty 1988, 225). Rorty has no difficulty admitting that we always remain under the "causal sway of something not ourselves" (1995, 192). In fact, he insists on it: "You cannot have any language, or any beliefs, without being in touch with both a human community *and* non-human reality" (Rorty 2021, 70). Problems arise only when we decide to interpret the causal pressure of reality in some determinate intentional (including representational) terms. The pressures are there, but they can be described in different ways for different purposes at different times (1999, 33), and there can be no ultimate manual for translating the non-intentional causal pressures into an intentional discursive idiom, adjudicating the choice between competing promising candidates.

According to Rorty, there is only one sensible way to resolve this conundrum: instead of validating our theories by trying to tie them to the conditions of their origination, we can switch attention to what happens when we attempt to carry them forward. Instead of wondering whether the content of a hypothesis can be faithfully traced to the event it was meant to explain, we can wonder whether it can help us answer more new questions about this event and events of a similar sort. Instead of the origin (in past reality), we can focus on the proposal's fertility – for transforming reality and our understanding thereof.

The advantage of the latter sort of question consists in being susceptible to receiving a plain kind of causal, practical answer: Our theory may be good for our intended purposes, or it may not work. Some theories will work better than others for certain purposes; meaning that, without being substantially more correct, they will fare better by producing more interesting results. These questions of being-fit-for-a-purpose, of being more productive under the conditions at hand, is all the sense of adequacy that we might actually need, in Rorty's view; and they can all be answered without dealing with the impossible question of "which is closer to reality" (Rorty 1988, 220).

For the traditional idea of being answerable to an unmediated, uninterpreted reality Rorty substitutes a sense of rational answerability to other human beings, in the face of causal pressures. Justification, as a prerequisite to knowledge, is not a matter of a relation between objects and ideas but rather of complex social practices (Rorty 1979, 170); with the intersubjective consensus of the qualified participants replacing the notion of objectivity, understood as a privileged relation to a nonhuman absolute (Rorty 2021, 16).

Being right is a matter of "victory in argument rather than of relation to an object known" (Rorty 1979, 156); and only "overattention to fact-stating" would prompt us to believe that, in addition to justification, our inquiries must also aim at some separate value called "truth" (Rorty 2021, 50). Our need for justification, in turn, requires no justification (Rorty 2021, 63). Our search of coherence, in our own beliefs and with candidate beliefs espoused by others, is driven by a need to avoid cognitive dissonance (Rorty 2021, 68–69). Our curiosity leads us to expand our horizons, creating the need to explain and defend our views in a coherent fashion in the light of new evidence, new considerations, and new differences of opinion. We aim to be ever more convincing to intelligent, informed, and critical interlocutors, without imaging that there must be some special mode of argument to seal a universal agreement (Rorty 2021, 72). When all the relevant parties are presently convinced beyond reasonable doubt, we call the resulting conviction "knowledge"; until, that is, some relevant cause disturbs the established consensus.

The notion of representation can still be legitimately employed under these constraints. However, it can no longer be regarded as a matter of capturing or matching some antecedent content by reference to which the accuracy of the resulting representation can be confirmed. Instead, it must be construed as a matter of learning how to engage in practices the skillful execution of which entitles one to rightfully claim to have engaged in a successful representation. Historical competence, historical literacy, for example, consists of a capacity to coherently imagine a past form of life on the basis of available evidence. Our conceptual norms for how reconstructions of this sort are to be accomplished stem not from the (impossible) acquaintance with the past that is being described, but from the analysis and examination of past historical narratives that are presently consensually judged to be both successful and exemplary.

Such norms are approximate and provisional but they provide us with enough "legible stabilities" (Margolis 2021, 273), to sustain a rigorous "realistic" form of praxis, qualified by an appropriate degree of plasticity and improvisation. Most importantly, while applied prospectively, these norms are essentially retrospective; they are answerable to the past practice rather than past reality: Reality is causal; but the norms for representing it are historical.

Productive growth requires balancing the demands of stabilizing legibility and experimental plasticity: "the need for consensus and the need for novelty" (Rorty 2007, 85). The former, in Rorty's terms, is meant to be addressed by epistemology – a theory of settled epistemic practices; the latter, by hermeneutics – a theory of unsettled interpretation (Rorty 1979, 321).[8] Epistemology deals with the aspects of discourse where it is appropriate to describe things in terms of "getting it right," simply because the relevant norms of judgment – settled in part by common sense, and in part by the pertinent expert cultures – currently benefit from a nearly universal acceptance (Rorty 2007, 124). All qualified participants are clear about the shared rules of the game. In areas of inquiry where this is predominantly the case – Rorty's examples are paleontology, particle physics, and epigraphy – solving problems does, in fact, resemble solving complicated puzzles, with the successful solutions being commonly recognized as "getting it right" (Rorty 2007, 181).

The limitation of the epistemological approach consists in being unable to countenance, on its own terms, the possibility of alternative cogent approaches and systems of norms, without reducing them to a version of one's own commitments and procedures. To the extent that such a reduction is possible, the alternative vocabulary appears superfluous; to the extent that it is not, at least partially erroneous. Rorty's response is simple: "if A can explain what she is doing and why she is doing it in her own terms, what right does B got to keep on saying, 'No, what A is *really* doing is . . . '?"[9] The hermeneutic dimension enables us to accept the possibility that someone may have a valid perspective and good reasons for holding it without sharing our epistemological common ground. It is more concerned with mutual respect and civility than with an uncontestable demonstration (Rorty 1979, 318–319); it also concedes that, by learning to see or describe things in new unfamiliar ways, we may be exposed to

[8] Rorty compares these to "normal" and "abnormal" discourse in the Kuhnian sense (ibid, 346).

[9] Cit. Voparil 2022, 161.

the significant features of our subject matter that we would have inevitably missed otherwise.

The extent of the radical alterity in these cases should not be overstated. Even a poetic innovation "typically requires the use of familiar, traditional, literal language" (Rorty 2001, 153). In this sense, the hermeneutic, interpretive dimension within any sufficiently developed field of inquiry is always reliant on the "normal" established epistemological consensus, from which it means to depart.[10] We push against the shore we aim to leave behind. Participating in a conversation requires prior acculturation; so, we begin by "finding out a lot about the descriptions of the world" endorsed by our culture (Rorty 1979, 365). "Every sphere of discourse," as Rorty points out, "– moral, scientific, mathematical, literary – has, so to speak, certain admission requirements, certain credentials which have to be presented before one is taken seriously" (2020, 186). One needs to acquire certain historical literacy, proficiency with collecting historical evidence, with deploying historically persuasive argumentation, before one can properly count as offering an alternative historical interpretation.

One aspect of the problem of significant interpretive differences can be addressed by distinguishing between the "projects of individual self-development" (Rorty 2007, 235) and the public concern with maintaining a reliable and truthful historical record. "Public," as Dewey perspicuously explains, is not merely "social" (LW.2.244): instead, it refers to a concern with the transactions that affect our "common interests" in such a way as to warrant a continuous and systematic monitoring and care in the interest of all (LW.2.246). Insofar as historical record possesses a public significance, the intended contributions must address the prevailing standards of the historical profession – entrusted with the care of this record – if only to contest them, in the name of a more adequate conception of common interest. In private and on the periphery of the public concern (say, in the case of an historical novel), such epistemological constraints become less pressing. But at the center of the public arena, even as we commit to encouraging the "experimentalist tinkering" (Rorty 2007, 86), we cannot waive one's "responsibility for making imaginative suggestions plausible," by explaining how they offer new solutions to old problems (Rorty 2007, 85) and defending their public utility (Rorty 2007, 86).

The other aspect, the conflict of interpretations in the absence of common interest – especially, in the context of an open power struggle – is considerably more complicated. In such cases, the divergent traditions may endorse or emphasize somewhat different norms of historical epistemic evaluation, focusing on the ones that favor the championed cause or account, to the extent that

[10] Comp. Rorty 1979, 365.

a particular way of narrating history may become intimately fused with the sense of one's cultural identity.

An historian, then, often deals with an essentially contested social reality, where the problem of interpretation is compounded by the problem of conflicting historical allegiances. Sometimes referred to in connection with the "crisis of representation" (Berkhofer 1997, 3) or the crisis of historical objectivity (Novick 1999, 523), the difficulty stems from the fact that there is no innocent, "natural" way to represent events as "they really are" without effectively choosing a side in an ideological debate. And while no one seriously believes that, in lieu of "absolute objectivity," one is left with "totally arbitrary interpretations" (Appleby, Hunt, Jacob 1994, 246); it can be quite difficult to provide a philosophical account of how the practical historical judgment is actually made once the old "representational matching" paradigm is dissolved. Rorty's holistic theory-comparison approach may sound attractive; but requires more context for a proper evaluation.

3.3 On the Uses of History

The Western philosophical tradition, according to Rorty, has always proceeded on the assumption that it must be possible to tell one big internally coherent story containing the answers to all our questions, fitted together into some sort of universal "jigsaw puzzle" (Rorty 2007, 80). However, this view is incompatible with the realization that human beings can sometimes rationally espouse genuinely incommensurable values. Because these values inform the general direction of our cognitive efforts, they give rise to at least partially incompatible perspectives – amenable to practical compromise but incapable of being unified into a seamless whole (Rorty 2007, 82). Rorty's solution to this problem is to declare ourselves "commonsensical finitists" – people who admit that they can only "solve old problems by creating new ones" (Rorty 2007, 88) and have no way of establishing with certainty, "at any given moment in history, whether humanity is heading in the right direction" (Rorty 2016, 57).

With respect to history, this implies that we may no longer be interested in developing a universal scheme of explanation, fulfilling (in the words of de Certeau) a "totalizing function" (De Certeau, 80), and might instead show more interest in *experimenting* with various explanatory models, exploring different configurations of enabling conditions and their limitations. A pragmatist history, then, abandons the essentialist commitments of the grand philosophical histories of the past, retaining, nevertheless their central emancipatory aspirations (Rorty 1998a, 230), construed in terms of "an exalted sense of new possibilities opening up for finite beings" (2010, 14). A pragmatist conception of the past, therefore, is future-oriented. The meaning of the past always remains interpretively indeterminate, until brought into contact with the animating interests of the present, which are, in turn, a product of our tentative and passing attempts to answer the question of: What can we reasonably hope for?

Instead of focusing on "getting things right" (whatever that might mean), Rorty advises us to pursue the open-ended project of "enlarging our repertoire of individual and cultural self-descriptions" (2007, 124); and, instead of trying to winnow them down so as to disclose some underlying unchanging shared core, to celebrate and collect the ways in which "we differ from our ancestors" and ones in which "our descendants might differ from us" (2007, 182). Instead of digging deeper in order to discover something higher, we need to think *horizontally*: expanding our conception of the human potential, exemplified in its profound diversity by the historical record. Our quest for autonomy, for emancipation, for self-determination, on this particular view, finds its highest expression (following Nietzsche) in our capacity to transform ourselves into something new (Rorty 2016, 31); and history serves this function by expanding our conception of viable options.

Rather than seeking to increase the coherence of our current intuitions and ways of picturing a meaningful human life in the midst of a growing, developing world, we should follow Emerson in believing that every description of things, no matter how warranted, must eventually be transcended and replaced by another (Rorty 2016, 7), and attempt to imagine promising alternatives to our present perspective and mindset. Rationality, says Rorty, "is a matter of making allowed moves within language games. Imagination creates the games that reason proceeds to play" (Rorty 2016, 15). But imagination, of course, is not beholden to either truth or goodness (Rorty 2016, 55) and, in part because of this, it makes sense to suggest – although Rorty himself does not – that historical, cultural imagination could benefit from being adequately informed by, and perhaps even rooted in, historical reality.

The overall thrust, in short, of the proposed pragmatist revision to the traditional philosophical attitudes is to advance towards curiosity and away from complacency and egotistic self-contentment: "to embrace more and more possibilities" (Rorty 1991, 154), while letting go of established identities and narratives that support them (Marchetti 2022, 69). As Paul Roth points out, "logical possibilities for action" are much more affected by our ways of thinking about and describing things than natural phenomena (2020, 40). For Rorty, we choose our existential paths and justify our values by "telling a story" about the possible historical worlds in which those values would be realized (2020, 21). In this sense, one could say that the proliferation of such narratives creates new distinctive ways of being, and makes the emergence of a certain type of person possible; in the best cases, leading to the formation of novel (experimental) but fluently functional selves. The whole point of high culture, in Rorty's exaggerated phrase, consists in sorting past visions and figures into good and bad ones (Rorty 1982, 65), separating "the sort of person one wants to be from the sort one does not want to be" (1989, 47). To put it more modestly, one of the most important functions of historical culture is to enable us to explore our affinities and tensions with respect to the various concrete manifestations of the shared human potential.

To the extent that history can be seen as a product of "specifically human choices," one of the more compelling reasons for examining our past arises from the desire to mediate a "responsible transition from present to future" (White 1966, 132–133). In a culture that had succeeded in shedding the last vestiges of the Platonic predilection for eternal forms, "history rather than science, philosophy, art, or literature" would become central to intellectual life; providing the same benefits for each new human generation that "conversation with those who have lived long and seen much offers to the young" (Rorty 2016, 59). But what we are meant to learn from this accumulated historical cultural experience, ironically, is how to make "human future very different from the human past" (Brandom 2021, xxix). Experience teaches us how to go on experimenting with no sublime purpose or end in sight: "to move things about, rearrange them so as to highlight their relations to other things, in the hope of finding ever more useful, and therefore ever more beautiful, patterns" (Brandom 2021, xxxiv). This finitist, experimental posture implies that we cannot approach history with some antecedently established scale of values (moral, or otherwise), by which to judge progress and condemn failure. All we can count on, according to Rorty, are specific comparisons between concrete historical alternatives (Rorty 1990, 211), towards which we find ourselves differentially disposed.

In lieu of secure philosophical foundations, there is no reason to persist in "the game of pretending that there is something above and beyond human history that can sit in judgment on that history" (Rorty 2022, 42). We can attempt to justify our culture and our modes of social organization only by drawing historical comparisons to other cultures and modes of social organization (Rorty 1989, 53): and if "the study of history cannot convince" our opponents, "nothing else can do so" (Rorty 2022, 42). Moral insight, which informs our cultural perspectives, cannot be a product of abstract rational reflection: It is rather a matter of being able to imagine a better future and of conducting practical experiments to explore the various possibilities on offer (Rorty 2022, 47). Instead of continuing the futile search for unassailable philosophical foundations we must be simply prepared to "learn from the historical record" (Rorty 2022, 48).

Different values and different purposes that animate the competing philosophical perspectives boil down, in practice, to "a choice among groups of people rather than a choice among abstract formulae" (Rorty 2022, 24). These "loyalties and convictions" which express our hopes for the future of humanity and constitute, simultaneously the basis of our self-understanding, overlap with the convictions of some social and cultural groups and contrast with others; and the moral and perspectival dilemmas we face stem from the fact that "most of us identify with a number of different communities," and when these communities are in conflict we are usually reluctant to sever our ties to any of them (Rorty 1990, 201). Historical comparisons between different forms of life cannot always settle these conflicts of value and perspective; nor do they always settle them in the way that we find to be appropriate and desirable. Still, they are all that we are legitimately entitled to; while pretending to have some immaculate philosophical convictions to ground our practical preferences is merely a conventional, rhetorically effective way of combining pedantry with dishonesty.

This deflationary conclusion squares well, moreover, with Rorty's rather prosaic, biologistic conception of cultural dynamics. "The history of human social practices," according to him, "is continuous with the history of biological evolution" by natural selection (Rorty 1998a, 206). Culturally gifted individuals are merely "experiments in living" (Rorty 1989, 45), peculiar "causal products of natural forces" (Rorty 1989, 28). Their utterances – the ideas and the stories they produce – can be conceived on the analogy with biological genes, as artifacts of a partially faithful replication of some preexisting cultural forms, occasionally enriched by the serendipitous errors in translation. We could as well ascribe their genesis to the "scrambling" of some atoms by "cosmic rays" (Rorty 1989, 17). Only some of these fortuitous productions catch on, and their effects are, consequently, amplified through propagation. "Our language and our culture," says Rorty, "are as much a contingency, as much a result of thousands of small mutations finding niches (and millions of others finding no niches), as are the orchids and the anthropoids" (Rorty 1989, 16). The contributions that become important (or even transformative) do not owe their success to capturing a precious aspect of some deeper reality; they merely satisfy some transient need due to "the contingencies of some historical situation" (Rorty 1989, 37). Their cultural prominence is a result of an "accidental coincidence of a private obsession with a public need" (Rorty 1989). In Chris Voparil's apt characterization, they do not function as "mirrors" representing profound truths, but merely as "levers" capable of altering the cultural conversation due to their strategic placement (Voparil 2004, 222 & 227).

Most of these cultural innovations will have their "utility explained only retrospectively" (Rorty 1989, 55), and the eventual recognition may be long in waiting. The question of whether their eventual acceptance is due to genuinely "good reasons" or the purely contingent "historical reasons," moreover, cannot be answered: The line between the proper reasons and inadvertent causes being hopelessly blurred (Rorty 1989, 48). The advantage of such a "naturalist" conception of cultural development, in Rorty's opinion, consists in teaching us "to see a blind impress as not unworthy of programming our lives or our poems" (Rorty 1989, 55). Therefore, he remains sanguine in the face of the criticisms that theories of this sort leave our collective cultural history at the mercy of "language-creating protuberances" (Habermas 1992, 206). Rorty is fascinated with personal stories of contingent individual development; but he is deliberately wary of any philosophical stories of systematic cultural renewal that may be offered to supplement them (Rorty 1989, 101).

Ideally, in a democratic society, Rorty maintains, human beings must be in charge of shaping their own history, with no authority but themselves to show them the path (1998, 18). The prospect of living without authoritative philosophical reassurances may well be unsettling, but it is better and more honest than trading in the illusions of speculative certainty. We need not delude ourselves, moreover, by an unconditional trust in the popular will: ignorance, narrow-mindedness, and bias that fuel the successive waves of populism are both real and wide-spread. However, we can still hope that "the people will someday come to their senses" (Rorty 2022, 107). Until that day, our public concerns remain squarely political: to prevent the oppression of the weak by the strong, to ensure the equality of opportunity and social justice (Rorty 2022, 106). In Rorty's opinion, as long as we remedy the disparities of political power, culture can eventually take care of itself (Rorty 2022, 92), without any special philosophical dispensations.

Meanwhile, we have no reason to judge the worth of the democratic institutions "by the sort of person they create," even if the resulting characters are bland, petty, and unheroic (Rorty 1990, 190). Personal, individual development is a private matter (in a sense proposed earlier) but freedom and tolerance are the essential concerns of the public (Brandom 2021, xxxi). A democratic society is like a "bazaar" where "you smile a lot" and "make the best deals you can" (Rorty 1990, 209). For the traditional conception of cultural education as a way of attaining a full and proper realization of one's intrinsic humanity, Rorty is ready to substitute a nondirectional ideal of "aesthetic enhancement" (Rorty 1979, 13) which can be furthered, for example, by acquainting oneself with "some exotic culture or historical period" or simply spontaneously "thinking up" new words and aims (Rorty 1979, 360). Accordingly, he is prepared to treat history as "a collection of anecdotes" or "cautionary tales" rather than "a coherent dramatic narrative" (Rorty 1998a, 240 & 242).

Rorty's nonchalant commitment to treating history as a series of inspirational tales has prompted others to question whether his theory may possibly entail a refusal "to face up to the unsightly realities of our past" (Voparil 2004, 235) or to live with "the cognitive dissonance that results from accepting aspects of our history we would rather forget while not forgetting aspects we can still respect" (Warnke 2021, 241), suggesting the conclusion that his sense of history is "too broad, too thin, devoid of realities of power" (West 1989, 207). This is a fair charge and a good reason to believe that a pragmatist philosophy of history requires something more than the pluralism and openness rightly championed by Rorty.

On the one hand, there is no good reason why history needs to be integrated into a single coherent and timeless narrative. We value the outstanding contributions of great individual historians precisely on the account of their distinctive, peculiar manner of handling, interpreting, and arranging historical materials. The contemporary relevance of Tacitus or Michelet cannot be measured simply by their contribution to the objectively complete account of the past. Their relevance, instead, is secured by their *difference*: by their characteristic style – completely impossible for a working historian of today – yet, so stunningly representative of their own intellectual, historical epoch and surroundings. After all, an important part of history, and being a historian, consists in coming to terms with the historiographical tradition and the transformations of cultural, and historical consciousness reflected therein.

Acquiring new points of view, reimagining the present and the past from different, potentially clashing perspectives, broadens our intellectual horizons in an essential and indispensable manner; and Rorty's incisive assessment of the philosophically entrenched notions of correspondence and conceptual unity opens the door to a positive appreciation of historical fragmentation and perspectival dispersion.

However, his accompanying deflationary naturalistic reduction of cultural agency to pure contingency, with the production of novel cultural possibilities ascribed to unspecified constellations of "causal forces," their retrospective value established by the contextual peculiarities of their successful reception, appears both unwarranted and philosophically unproductive. Successful reception is an ambivalent criterion of enduring cultural value. Similarly, an ongoing generation of contingent perspectival differences, betting that some of them may prove unexpectedly enlightening in the process of retrospective filtration, is neither statistically promising, nor true to the way novel cultural perspectives are ordinarily brought into existence.

New perspectives usually arise as a result of concerted inquiry, a sustained effort to solve a problem or articulate a point of view. Novel metaphors that have a transformative influence on our imaginations and our vocabularies, are not mere linguistic protuberances of uncertain provenance, they are illuminating analogies, which (it is true) are usually happened upon by chance. But the inspiration only comes to the one who labors in earnest to accomplish a greater insight and understanding. Promising modes of expression, transformative perspectives arise from an intelligent response to some cultural or existential situation; and the reason that we treat them with interest in the first place has to do with the fact that they succeed at being representative of a distinctive aspect of the human condition. Because of this, Emerson's and Dewey's sustained engagements with the problem of representativeness discussed above seem more philosophically promising than Rorty's own distinctively laissez-faire attitude.

Rorty's resistance to offering special philosophical criteria for cultural advancement is not without merit; however, to the extent that it signals a reluctance to engage in a certain kind of theoretical discussions, its positing of causal contingency as the sole mechanism of cultural development undermines the motivation for historical cultural reflection – an intellectual practice often regarded as central to social criticism, historical learning, and cultural progress. On a more balanced pragmatist view, history performs both a decentering and an integrative conceptual function. Moving forward, it introduces new differentiations, complications, so as to reflect the diversity of the changing forms of life and evolving theoretical concerns. In the moments of normative, reflective recollection it consolidates its previous findings in as systematic a form as its presently assembled materials allow.

As Dewey points out, a student appreciates the great historical systems at least as much "for the meanings and shades of meanings they have brought to light" (LW.1.306), as for the specific truths that they helped us to ascertain. An important question for pragmatism, offering a suitable opening for the next, closing chapter, is "whether inquiry can develop in its own ongoing course the logical standards and forms to which further inquiry shall submit" (LW.12.13). In other words, can historical research become the ultimate source of its own guiding norms?

4 Brandom on Representation and Historical Recollection

As Paul Roth observes, contemporary philosophy is indebted to Thomas Kuhn for convincing us that "what passes as scientific rationality has a history" (Roth 2020, 19). Robert Brandom, in turn, can be credited with developing a persuasive model for articulating the relationship between such histories and the (successive) conceptions of the pertinent aspects of reality they give rise to. Research traditions – traditions of inquiry, in the classical pragmatist vocabulary – consolidate themselves over time around certain central presuppositions regarding their subject matter, certain methodological norms and procedures; a core of central analytic concepts; a number of exemplary problems, cases; paradigmatic figures, studies, solutions. Yet, what they claim to represent, in the end, is truth, reality. Historians, specifically, claim to tell us the truth about the past, to represent what had actually happened. Brandom's account assists us in redeeming this claim in terms of a progressive articulation of the originally intended subject matter, without claiming an (impossible) privileged access to an antecedent reality independent of our historically developing (sometimes conflicting) perspectives. The Dorian invasion refers to some past reality, but what we mean by it is liable to change over time; we learn more about it despite continually moving away from it; and there is a warranted disagreement about what it actually was (because, at the very least, it was a number of things). Yet, there is a historical tradition which accepts the content of this concept as real and claims that we can genuinely understand more about it, without ever being able to encounter it as such. Brandom's expressivist pragmatism enables us to formulate a rational account of this somewhat puzzling circumstance.

Truth, of course, is what we ultimately aim at and, because of this, our use of concepts has an important representational dimension. But "truth" and "representation," according to Brandom, are not the best terms for explaining how our concepts gain their meaning; instead, it is representation itself that requires analysis and explanation. "Inference" gives us a better starting point, with a true assertion being one that serves as "an appropriate *premise* from which to make *inferences*" (Brandom 2009, 168), and the adequate grasp of its meaning turning into "a question about which inferences to endorse" Brandom 2009, 123). To understand what a statement means is to understand what would follow from it (if true): that is, how it affects the relevant patterns of reasoning or inference. In deciding on the truth of a statement about the past, for example, we would no longer worry about its accuracy in describing some temporal episode to which we no longer have access but would wonder instead "what follows from such claims, what do they preclude, what would be evidence for or against them" (Brandom 2009, 172). If the emperor was assassinated on a certain date, there should be no genuine records of his (earthly) activities conducted after that date. If there are such records, then either the emperor had not been assassinated, or the records are false, or the postmortem emperor was, in fact, an impostor. Each one of these hypothetical possibilities, in turn, gives rise to further chains of implication that may become evidentially corroborated or compromised in the course of investigation. The patterns of inference that accord best with the *presently* available evidence confer upon their main constituent statements the status of a warranted candidacy for truth.

There are two complimentary ways in which this basic inferential intuition can be explicated further. To begin with, the concern with truth, here, has been replaced with a question of what really follows from or is incompatible with what (Brandom 2019, 435).[11] The growth of experience produces friction between the consequences of our preexisting commitments, forcing us to refine their meaning and their truth-status. A person who finds herself with incompatible commitments "has the experience of error" (Brandom 2019, 76). For instance, one reliable report confirms the emperor's successful assassination, while another details his subsequent involvement in the affairs of the state. Importantly, the only reason that we can regard these two reports or commitments as incompatible is that we do assume them to pertain to (or represent) the same underlying state of affairs (Brandom 2019). The recognition of the candidate commitments' incompatibility is premised on the assumption of their subject-matter's unitary, noncontradictory reality. In competition, these descriptions are posited provisionally as different "modes of presentation" of the same (Brandom 2019, 78); until one (or both of them) are shown to be mere appearances in relation an improved and refined commitment regarding what really happened (e.g., the assassination was staged).

Every empirical descriptive concept or statement, according to Brandom, has "modal consequences" (Brandom 2015, 67): rendering certain things more and others less possible. This need not be a matter of strict logical necessity, but more frequently of what Brandom calls "materially good inferences," which hold in virtue of their nonlogical (usually empirical) contents (2000, 37): "if I let loose of the leash, the dog will chase the cat" (Brandom 2015, 192). Such probative inferences are usually defeasible, meaning that they only hold provided certain conditions or ceteris paribus clauses, and no one supposes that all the pertinent conditions of their appropriate application could ever be spelled out in final, rigorous ways (Brandom 2015, 164). Nevertheless, within a concrete situation, these inferences start generating, however provisionally, "a space of possibilities structured by relations of compatible and incompatible differences," which initially endow our experience with determinate meaning (Brandom 2019, 141).

[11] Brandom traces many of his commitments, in this regard, to Hegel. In what follows, these attributions are omitted to simplify the exposition by avoiding the complicated problems of philosophical reconstruction and genealogy.

"Describing something in the actual situation," according to Brandom, "*always* involves substantial commitments as to how it *would* behave, or what else *would* be true of it, in other *possible* situations," including the counterfactual ones (Brandom 2015, 68). We assert, for example, that the record cannot be patently false because, had it been, given its wide circulation and conspicuous subject matter, it would have almost certainly been discredited by knowledgeable contemporaries. Merely applying a descriptive label without considering its inferential implications does not tell us what something is actually being described *as*. A contemporary event can be equally well described as a "mutiny" or a "revolution"; and we cannot rationally decide between these descriptions without considering the consequences of applying one, rather than another. A competent description is inseparable from an inferentially articulated conception of the event and, in this sense, from an at least incipient explanation.

As we compare the inferential implications of our explanatory descriptions with the implications of competing descriptions and the pertinent evidence arising in the course of our investigation, creatively eliminating the resulting incompatibilities and contradictions, we refine our initial conception of the subject matter, rendering it more determinate and differentiated. What awaits us at the ideal limit of this process? According to Brandom, it is the notion of what the thing in question "*ought* to be" for us (Brandom 2019, 435), what we *should* conceptualize it as. At any given point in time, it is simply the best rational account of it that we can provide; introducing the second, recollective and expressive part of the original inferentialist story.

"One treats one's currently endorsed conceptions and commitments as presenting the reality behind prior appearances," says Brandom (2019, 437); and it is in relation to the subject matter as presently conceived that the earlier conceptions of it assume the familiar guise of incomplete, partially adequate, or merely approximate representations. Our current view, however, must be rationally vindicated vis-à-vis these earlier representations to deserve its privilege status, charting an "expressive genealogy" (Brandom 2019, 437) that convincingly explains how the present conception *fulfills* the intention of the earlier ones by appropriately resolving the problems and contradictions they have generated in the course of subsequent experience and learning.

At the outset – for example, when trying to understand what underlies the references to the Dorian invasion – what one intends "exceeds what one can presently grasp"; yet, introducing some initial characterization of the subject matter already renders one answerable (in inferential terms) for all the complications that the subject matter thus introduced may eventually accrue (Brandom 2019, 408). Retrospectively, we say that what the initial generic description intended is what we now have found out by following its direction, even when our findings consist in discovering that the initial description was substantially wrong. Similarly, a person who tells us to look for the castle at the end of the path remains answerable to our eventual finding that the structure at the end of the path is actually a barn. Retrospectively, the path from the initial suggestion to the present determination is one of discovery (Brandom 2019, 6); but prospectively, it is a path of invention (Brandom 2019, 7), of conjecture, of trial and error, of devising ingenious ways of incorporating new evidence and overcoming accumulated incompatibilities and contradictions.

This basic outline, of course, requires substantial filling out. At its center, stands the pragmatist contention that the conceptual norms governing our assessment of the correctness of proposed solutions (and representations) can only be developed in the course of a successful practical engagement with the concrete subject matter. The norms and methods of inquiry, in the end, are simply ways of "codifying some sort of knowing *how* in the form of knowing *that*" (Brandom 2000, 8). Importantly, one can accomplish a practical mastery of the subject matter, without developing an awareness of the theoretical significance of one's mode of proceeding (Brandom 2002, 87).

The reverse, however, does not hold – we cannot substitute the knowledge of epistemic norms and principles for the practical capacity of an expert judgment. Pragmatists, including Brandom, tend to construe *experience* (as a learning process) in terms of an "adaptive attunement to the environment" (Brandom 2011, 7). Moreover, they conceive of experience in active experimental terms, "with representing and intervening understood as correlated processes" (Brandom 2011, 54), with the hypothetical assignments of meaning (interpretations) continuously tested against the progressively uncovered materials that stand in need of an explanation.

The meaning of concepts derives from their "use," from applying them in specific judgments (Brandom 2011, 638); with all the determinateness that a concept has resulting from a history of its application (Brandom 2011, 361). That said, it may still be difficult to see how a practice of employing a concept or a cognitive rule could, all by itself, "institute a norm that is sufficiently determinate to serve as a standard of correctness for an indefinite number of further possible uses" (Brandom 2011, 652).

Following his own pragmatist interpretation of Hegel, Brandom claims that concepts and norms gain their content in virtue of the role they play in "a tradition of actual use," configured by the process of recollection into a progressively expressive historical structure (Brandom 2002, 48 and 2019, 131). The best way to understand their proper meaning, in Rorty's paraphrase, "is to tell a story about ways in which the uses of certain words have changed in the past, leading up to a description of the different ways in which these words are being used now" (Rorty 2016, 41). Telling such stories, in turn, helps us realize that "objective criteria do not drop down from heaven but are themselves historical products" (Rorty 2016, 49).

A tradition of inquiry – an intellectual tradition, thus understood – offers us an ordered succession of perspectives, meant to exhibit an aspect of significant growth or progress over time. The nontrivial differences and even conflicts between the successive and alternative contemporaneous perspectives complicate mutual comprehension without, however, undermining it in a genuinely threatening way. In fact, their conflicts and incompatibilities only become intelligible against the background presumption of a shared subject-matter: and, as long as we maintain a general shared sense of "what is being talked about," we usually can bridge the difference in perspectives, successfully extracting "information across the doxastic gap" (Brandom 2000, 181). Nevertheless, this conception of subject-matter as something that all the perspectives within the tradition are aiming to represent, prevents us from being able to specify what is being thus represented. Everyone is offering views about "something," which itself remains unnamed, apart from the things that are being said about it.

The construal of a tradition as progressively expressive gives us a recipe for addressing this concern. To the extent that we treat the later pronouncements in a tradition as substantial improvements over the earlier ones, we can say that the earlier construals were partial representations, or sequential appearances, of what is represented in our latest and most adequate conception of their underlying reality (Brandom 2019, 682). In specifying this reality, we cannot do better than the best vocabulary we currently possess – even as we admit that our present designations of the real will be relegated to the status of a mere representation, once the next superior way of discussing the reality in question becomes available. Until then, we interpret the past perspectives within the tradition to which we belong by determining what they "would be true of, if they were true" within our own current conception of the world (Brandom 2000, 182). So, for example, we say that the "morning star" and the "evening star" are *really* the planet Venus.

So, in the first place, one needs to be able to show "how the previous views one held in the process leading up to the current candidate can properly be understood as views, appearances, or representings *of* what one now endorses as the reality" (Brandom 2019, 680). But, beyond that, one must also "show how one *found out* that they are so," thereby explaining the origin of one's own perspective as a result of a learning process (Brandom 2019), rather than an arbitrary conceptual innovation. In order to do so and to construe the past perspectives as partially truth-bearing appearances, one must connect them, on the one hand, to the conceptual relations currently endorsed, while simultaneously exposing their "internal instabilities" (Brandom 2009, 101) that our present conception can successfully resolve. The resulting triumphalist reconstructions – of a tradition as a progressive learning process – tend to exclude, by their very nature, everything but the positive contributions to the growth of eventual understanding, with errors admitted only insofar as they prove instructive in the end (Brandom 2019, 685). Meanwhile, the actual process of "determining conceptual contents is characterized by discontinuities, caesurae, radical reassessment of old commitments, and the unraveling of previous progress" (Brandom 2009, 103). This unaccounted for residue, however, has its own positive role to play: for it gives rise to the alternative reconstructions and subsequent criticisms of the established tradition (Brandom 2019, 746).

Why should a systematic learning process assume the form of a (reconstructed) historical tradition? Following Kant, philosophers tend to construe the norms of rationality in terms of systematicity (Brandom 2019, 68): Our commitments are held to be logically answerable to other commitments we hold and remain consistent with them. Hegel, then, reinterpreted these relations of rational answerability in social and historical terms, with successive stages of historical and intellectual tradition responsible for and to each other. Thus, we maintain an obligation to the future to responsibly administer our intellectual inheritance, to the demands and norms of which we hold ourselves answerable.

Brandom, sometimes, compares this historical structure to the process of statute elaboration in common law (Brandom 2009, 84). The applicability of a rule (in a specific case) is determined by the historical precedent of earlier authoritative applications; and, to the extent that the present judgment is deemed justified in the light of this history, it comes to constitute a further precedent, authoritative for the future applications of the rule. Similarly, in historical writing, a competent contribution to the study of Renaissance, for example, is generally expected to incorporate and integrate the conclusions and the arguments of the previous authoritative contributions to the subject, in order to establish its own standing as a potentially authoritative rational extension of the earlier historical practice. This retrospective "synthesis by rational integration" (Brandom 2009, 85), which constitutes an intellectually authoritative tradition, is what Brandom, following Hegel, calls "recollection" (Brandom 2009, 16).

The resulting narrative examines previous commitments within the tradition as "partial, and only partially correct revelation of things as they are now known" (Brandom 2009, 100), providing, thereby, a constructively critical account of the past from the perspective of the present. In doing so, it also provides a rational justification for our present commitments by exhibiting them as an outcome of a rational learning process that involved developing and revising the most warranted and promising commitments of our predecessors in the light of the difficulties they have eventually engendered. Simultaneously, it creates a greater sense of stability and continuity of the actual referents of our central theoretical concepts, of a shared and partially (progressively) determinate subject matter that endures despite the differences of the pertinent theoretical perspectives.

In the social-historical context of a tradition, our claims to rationality and systematicity are vindicated not by an abstract logical standard of formal consistency but by an appeal to the considered judgment of qualified interlocutors. Our claims and arguments have many inferential consequences, but their significance can only be assessed within a proper context of justification, as appropriate moves within a rule-governed conversation. The same observation may have very different implications in the intellectual game of military history than it does in the game of meteorology. "Everything discovered," as Dewey once insisted, "belongs to the community of workers. Every new idea and theory has to be submitted to this community for confirmation and test" (LW 5.115). The abstract norms endorsed by a community (of professional historians, in our case) do not suffice, on their own, to endow one's utterances with determinate conceptual content, unless these norms are administered by the competent members of the intellectual community (Brandom 2019, 302). One cannot secure a genuine sense of belonging within the tradition by merely claiming to observe what one believes to be its governing norms. For instance, one does not become an historian merely by following the precepts of a recent respectable publication in historical theory.

In order to be responsible to the tradition in the right way, and in order for one's statements to enjoy the corresponding authority within the tradition, one must be recognized by the appropriately qualified others as one of their own, as a competent participant in the game. What one can do on their own, by following one's best understanding of the rules of engagement, is "*petition* others for recognition, in an attempt to become responsible or authoritative" (Brandom 2009, 70). We have a choice, of course, with respect to the traditions that we want to belong to and even, to some extent, with respect to choosing our guiding authorities within a particular tradition or a discipline. However, it is not up to us whether we qualify as "one of them" (Brandom 2019a, 45). In choosing the norms by which we aspire to measure our failure or success, we also choose to submit to the judgment of those who can rightfully claim to have an appropriate grasp of these norms; and while the moves that we make and the arguments we offer may be our own, their significance within an established tradition lies with the judgment of others, beyond our individual control (Brandom 2009, 72).

Sometimes, of course, the differences and the disagreements that arise within the tradition cannot be resolved simply on the basis of the commonly accepted norms. Dealing with genuine problems, incompatibilities, and contradictions is very often not a straightforward logical but a complicated practical matter; and there are always alternative means to securing one's goal (Brandom 2019, 444). For example, we can discredit one or both of the competing possibilities; or revise one or both in a number of suitable ways. Here, one is required to commit to a choice, thereby implicitly endorsing a conceptual, intellectual norm that some others within the tradition are not prepared to recognize.

Such parting of the ways is entirely normal, and need not at all imply that one party has got it "right" and the other has got it "wrong." Each one proceeds by somewhat different lights or norms. One may prove eventually to be unsustainable or emerge as clearly superior; or the two may become reconciled and integrated anew. All of these outcomes – including, of course, the continued coexistence of the two divergent traditions – are potentially valuable, but none are optimal. After all, according to Brandom, "one of the great goods for us is the availability of inexhaustible supply of new vocabularies in which to express, develop, constitute, and transform ourselves and our institutions, and for understanding the process by which we do that" (Brandom 2009, 150).

Because of this, Brandom explicitly reminds his fellow "tradition mongers" how limiting and distorting a view from within an established, well-integrated tradition may become (Brandom 2002, 91). An historical recollection that constitutes a tradition presents us with a retrospective story of how our present understanding of the subject-matter was progressively developed over time, creating the illusion that the whole time the developments within the tradition have been asymptotically approaching some antecedent reality, independent of interpretation and thought (Brandom 2019, 694).

When positioned at the end of a well-told story, it is tempting to mistake "one *aspect* of the process, one perspective on it, for the whole thing" (Brandom 2019, 442). Telling "*more* such stories" (Brandom 2002, 16), according to Brandom, is the best antidote we possess for such exclusivist illusions. We need to be "irenic, tolerant, and pluralistic": in Brandom's chosen words, to "let a hundred flowers blossom" (Brandom 2002, 104). In fact, one's mastery of the subject matter may be best measured by "the ability to *navigate* and *negotiate* between different perspectives" (Brandom 2002, 109).

"The more paths one knows through the wood," Brandom explains, "the better one knows one's way around it" (Brandom 2002, 115). Besides, to the extent that one aspires to reconstruct a tradition that is both comprehensive and inclusive, as opposed to parochial and narrow, one needs to learn to interpret charitably a wide array of divergent contributions, spanning long periods of time, animated by a broad range of changing cultural concerns, to be able to negotiate the differences between them, and to extract something valuable from every earnest and worthwhile perspective, including ones that are intellectually distant from one's own. Still, no perspective can aspire to be complete; no-reconstructed tradition, to be all-inclusive. There are real discontinuities and real incompatibilities, visible in the spaces between the integrated, continuous narratives constructed by the competing traditions (Brandom 2009, 113). It is from within these spaces that new narratives and alternative perspectives arise, perpetuating the possibility of intellectual renewal, experimentation, and reform.

To conclude, the process of retrospective recollection, of a systematic reconstruction of an intellectual tradition (a tradition of historical writing, for example) can help in establishing certain lines of conceptual continuity that assist in the process of learning as well as transfer of experience and understanding within the tradition. By focusing on "the process of experience by which all of our commitments, including those that address the relations among concepts, rationally and empirically develop" (Brandom 2009, 99), it contributes simultaneously to a sense of our own place within that process, of our present intellectual constitution and identity.

Self-consciousness can be a feature of traditions and disciplines, as well as persons. Self-conscious entities, of course, are distinguished from merely conscious ones by their capacity to transform themselves by forming new conceptions, or new understanding of themselves (Brandom 2009, 146). This can be accomplished in many ways. However, Brandom recommends one particular, modern form of historical self-consciousness: whereby we advance to the next stage of cultural, intellectual development by forming a recollectively integrated conception of the genesis of our present stage of inquiry or investigation (Brandom 2019, 470). To historians, this may suggest an idea of a systematic value of meta-history, of historical theory that aims to recapture the principles and commitments implicit in the past growth and development of the historical writing itself.

Conclusion

To conclude, one distinguishing feature of the pragmatist approaches to the problem of representation consists in their rejection of what Dewey once called "the spectator model" of encountering reality, preserved intact for eternity and admired respectfully from afar. Instead, pragmatists believe in engaging reality actively – in both practically and cognitively productive, transformative ways. This, in turn, requires a generally reliable understanding of how things are connected in the domain of interest, of what follows from what. Accordingly, pragmatists are usually inclined to favor some version of an inferentialist conception of truth, meaning, and conceptual content.

Contrary to the traditional idea of representation as correspondence, pragmatists argue that seeing something – even seeing it clearly and distinctly – does not amount to having an adequate understanding of what one sees. One must interpret the situation, and this normally requires grasping the representative, diagnostic significance of some of its constitutive elements, providing us with an indication of what is actually going on. Surface appearances do not all carry the same evidential weight. Because of this, the meaning of a situation is secured through an intelligent reconstruction based on reliable inferences from promising outward signs, not from just matching conventional terms or descriptive sentences to the apparent "facts." As Brandom's account suggests, a description is inseparable from an inferentially articulated conception of the event and, therefore, from an at least incipient explanation. One cannot count as telling the truth about the event, while offering a false or misleading explanation thereof.

Our relationship to representing the past, plays a special role in the pragmatist story. As cultural beings, we do not simply live in a natural world, but also in an interpreted world, where things and experiences are invested with complex meanings in virtue of past human activities and transactions.

Our intelligent engagement with the world depends not only on what the world is but on what we and others imagine and have imagined it to be: on possibilities that we recognize and those of which we remain unnecessarily ignorant. If our past, then, is conceptually structured as a space of mutually compatible or incompatible possibilities, then learning more about – and even reconceiving – our history changes the sense of what is possible and of what things actually mean in our partially inherited cultural world. Because of this, representative contributions – in action and thought; private and public; intended and unintended – transform our sense of what is possible and alter our expectations and valuations by shedding a new light on the structural conditions that enable and constrain their exercise, and the very possibility of their meaningful existence. History, from this perspective, bears witness to, and supplies resources for, the human struggle to articulate dignified and sustainable forms of living under an endless run of concrete historical situations.

This conception of history, of course, resonates well with the "practical idealism" shared by Emerson and Dewey, which recognizes all presently established forms of life as passing, and encourages an active commitment – in both the individual and the society – to a melioristic self-transformation, through learning and development rooted in the cultural, intellectual, historical tradition. Plausible reasons can be adduced in favor of maintaining such an attitude in a democratic society; but such an argument would go beyond the purview of the current brief. Meanwhile, the lesson with respect to historical representation shared by all the pragmatist figures we have discussed is simply this: The traditional conception of representation as correspondence has been constraining us in the wrong way – not in the way that good theories are constrained by data, but in the way that a conversation is constrained by an engrained unwarranted prejudice. By leaving its conventional empiricism behind in favor of a more probing, more experimental, and more pragmatist engagement with the historical experience, we do not lose scientific rigor and open-mindedness, we reclaim it.

Abbreviations

The following abbreviations are used to refer to the writing of Ralph Waldo Emerson:

EL	*The Early Lectures of Ralph Waldo Emerson*, 3 vols. (Cambridge, MA: Harvard University Press, 1959–72)
JMN	*Journals and Miscellaneous Notebooks of Ralph Waldo Emerson*, 16 vols. (Cambridge, MA: Belknap Press, 1960–1982)
LLR	*The Later Lectures of Ralph Waldo Emerson*, 2 vols. (Athens, GA: University of Georgia Press, 2010)
W	*The Complete Works of Ralph Waldo Emerson*, 12 vols. (Boston: Houghton Mifflin, 1903–4)

The following abbreviations are used for references to John Dewey's work as found in the standard critical edition:

EW	*John Dewey: The Early Works*, 5 vols. (Carbondale: Southern University Press, 1969–1972)
MW	*John Dewey: The Middle Works*, 14 vols. (Carbondale: Southern University Press, 1976–1988)
LW	*John Dewey: The Later Works*, 17 vols. (Carbondale: Southern University Press, 1981–1991)

References

Adams, H. (1918). *The Education of Henry Adams*. Cambridge, MA: Riverside Press.

Alexander, T. (1987). *John Dewey's Theory of Art, Experience, and Nature*. Albany, NY: SUNY Press.

Appleby, J., Hunt, L., and Jacob, M. (1994). *Telling the Truth about History*. New York: W. W. Norton.

Berkhofer, R. (1997). *Beyond the Great Story: History as Text and Discourse*. Cambridge, MA: Belknap Press.

Brandom, R. (2000). *Articulating Reasons: An Introduction to Inferentialism*. Cambridge, MA: Harvard University Press.

(2002). *Tales of the Mighty Dead*. Cambridge, MA: Harvard University Press.

(2009). *Reason in Philosophy: Animating Ideas*. Cambridge, MA: Belknap Press.

(2011). *Perspectives on Pragmatism: Classical, Recent, and Contemporary*. Cambridge, MA: Harvard University Press.

(2015). *From Empiricism to Expressivism*. Cambridge, MA: Harvard University Press.

(2019). *A Spirit of Trust: A Reading of Hegel's Phenomenology*. Cambridge, MA: Belknap Press.

(2019a). *Heroism and Magnanimity*. Milwaukee, WI: Marquette University Press.

(2021). Achieving the Enlightenment. In R. Rorty, ed., *Pragmatism as Anti-Authoritarianism*. Cambridge, MA: Belknap Press, vii–xxxv.

Burckhardt, J. (1979). *Reflections on History*. Indianapolis, IN: Liberty Classics.

De Certeau, M. (1988). *The Writing of History*. New York: Columbia University Press.

Dewey, J. (2012). *Unmodern Philosophy and Modern Philosophy*. Carbondale, IL: Southern Illinois University Press.

Dreon, R. (2022). *Human Landscapes: Contributions to a Pragmatist Anthropology*. Albany, NY: SUNY Press.

Friedl, H. (2000). Thinking America: Emerson and Dewey. In J. Raab, and R. Hagenbueche, eds., *Negotiations of America's National Identity*, Vol. 2. Tübingen: Stauffenburg, 131–157.

Habermas, J. (1992). *The Philosophical Discourse of Modernity*. Cambridge, MA: MIT Press.

Hickman, L. (2007). *Pragmatism as Post-Modernism: Lessons from John Dewey*. New York: Fordham University Press.

Hildebrand, D. (2003). *Beyond Realism and AntiRealism: John Dewey and the Neopragmatists*. Nashville, TN: Vanderbilt University Press.

(2008). *Dewey: A Beginner's Guide*. Oxford: Oneworld.

Kateb, G. (1994). *Emerson and Self-Reliance*. London: Sage.

Kuukkanen, J.-M. (2015). Postnarrativist *Philosophy of Historiography*. London: Palgrave Macmillan.

Lysaker, J. (2008). *Emerson and Self-Culture*. Bloomington, IN: Indiana University Press.

Marchetti, S. (2022). Bildung, Unimportance, and Moral Progress. In G. Marchetti, ed., *The Ethics, Epistemology, and Politics of Richard Rorty*. New York: Routledge, 64–82.

Margolis, J. (2021). *The Critical Margolis*. Albany, NY: SUNY Press.

Novick, P. (1988). *That Noble Dream: The "Objectivity Question" and the American Historical Profession*. Cambridge: Cambridge University Press.

Richardson, R. (1995). *Emerson: The Mind on Fire*. Berkeley, CA: University of California Press.

Robinson, D. (1993). *Emerson and the Conduct of Life: Pragmatism and Ethical Purpose in the Later Work*. Cambridge: Cambridge University Press.

Rorty, R. (1979). *Philosophy and the Mirror of Nature*. Princeton, TX: Princeton University Press.

(1982). *Consequences of Pragmatism*. Minneapolis, MN: University of Minnesota Press.

(1988). Representation, Social Practice, and Truth. *Philosophical Studies*, 54, 215–228.

(1989). *Contingency, Irony, and Solidarity*. Cambridge: Cambridge University Press.

(1990). *Objectivity, Relativism, and Truth*: *Philosophical Papers, Volume 1*. Cambridge: Cambridge University Press.

(1991). *Essays on Heidegger and Others, Volume 2*. Cambridge: Cambridge University Press.

(1992). *The Linguistic Turn: Essays in Philosophical Method*. Chicago, IL: University of Chicago Press.

(1995). Response to Frank Farrell. In H. Saatkamp, ed., *Rorty and Pragmatism: The Philosopher Responds to His Critics*. Nashville, TN: Vanderbilt University Press, 189–196.

(1996). Idealizations, Foundations, and Social Practices. In S. Benhabib, ed., *Democracy and Difference: Contesting the Boundaries of the Political*. Princeton, NJ: Princeton University Press, 333–335.

(1998). *Achieving Our Country*. Cambridge, MA: Harvard University Press.

(1998a). *Truth and Progress: Philosophical Papers, Volume 3*. Cambridge: Cambridge University Press.

(1999). *Philosophy and Social Hope*. New York: Penguin Books.

(2001). Response to Richard Shusterman. In M. Festenstein, and S. Thompson, eds., *Richard Rorty: Critical Dialogues*. Boston, MA: Polity Press, 153–157.

(2007). *Philosophy as Cultural Politics: Philosophical Papers, Volume 4*. Cambridge: Cambridge University Press.

(2010). *An Ethics for Today*. New York: Columbia University Press.

(2010a). *The Rorty Reader*. Boston, MA: Wiley-Blackwell.

(2014). *Mind, Language, and Metaphilosophy: Early Philosophical Papers*. Cambridge: Cambridge University Press.

(2016). *Philosophy as Poetry*. Charlottesville, VA: University of Virginia Press.

(2020). *On Philosophy and Philosophers: Unpublished Papers, 1960–2000*. Cambridge: Cambridge University Press.

(2021). *Pragmatism as Anti-Authoritarianism*. Cambridge, MA: Belknap Press.

(2022). *What Can We Hope For? Essays on Politics*. Princeton, TX: Princeton University Press.

Roth, P. (2020). *The Philosophical Structure of Historical Explanation*. Evanston, IL: Northwestern University Press.

Voparil, C. (2004). The Problem with Getting It Right. *Philosophy and Social Criticism*, 30, 221–246.

(2022). *Reconstructing Pragmatism: Richard Rorty and the Classical Pragmatists*. Oxford: Oxford University Press.

Warnke, G. (2021). Rorty and National Pride. In D. Rondel, ed., *The Cambridge Companion to Rorty*. Cambridge: Cambridge University Press, 222–242.

West, C. (1989). *The American Evasion of Philosophy*. Madison, WI: University of Wisconsin Press.

Whicher, S. (1953). *Freedom and Fate: An Inner Life of Ralph Waldo Emerson*. Philadelphia, PA: University of Pennsylvania Press.

White, H. (1966). The Burden of History. *History and Theory*, 5(2), 111–134.

Cambridge Elements

Historical Theory and Practice

Elements in the Series

Confronting Evil in History
Daniel Little

Progress and the Scale of History
Tyson Retz

Collaborative Historical Research in the Age of Big Data: Lessons from an Interdisciplinary Project
Ruth Ahnert, Emma Griffin, Mia Ridge and Giorgia Tolfo

A History of Big History
Ian Hesketh

Archaeology as History: Telling Stories from a Fragmented Past
Catherine J. Frieman

The Fabric of Historical Time
Zoltán Boldizsár Simon and Marek Tamm

Writing the History of Global Slavery
Trevor Burnard

Plural Pasts: Historiography between Events and Structures
Arthur Alfaix Assis

The History of Knowledge
Johan Östling and David Larsson Heidenblad

Conceptualizing the History of the Present Time
María Inés Mudrovcic

Writing the History of the African Diaspora
Toyin Falola

Pragmatism and Historical Representation
Serge Grigoriev

A full series listing is available at: www.cambridge.org/EHTP

Printed in the United States
by Baker & Taylor Publisher Services

Printed in the United States
by Baker & Taylor Publisher Services